Scouting in old picture postcards

by Jan van der Steen

European Library ZALTBOMMEL/THE NETHERLANDS

GB ISBN 90 288 1129 x

Second edition, 2000: reprint of the original edition of 1998.

European Library
post office box 49
NL – 5300 AA Zaltbommel/The Netherlands
telephone: 0031 418 513144
fax: 0031 418 515515
e-mail:publisher@eurobib.nl

Introduction

Scouting started in the early years of the 20th century. Originally it was meant to be a program for existing youth organizations, but spontaneously and totally unexpectedly boys all over Britain embraced the ideas and ideals and founded patrols and troops on their own. They improvised uniforms and went outdoors to track, camp, pioneer and do good turns. Girls followed in their tracks and claimed the same things. Two important facts added to the success of the formula: the founder, General Baden-Powell, was a national hero, known by everyone, and he was a gifted writer and illustrator. His book 'Scouting for Boys' became a bestseller overnight. Within one year he had sixty thousand young followers who caused almost chaos.

It would be difficult to imagine how these first Boy Scouts and Girl Guides looked and what they did in the early years of the movement if not for another phemomenon: the picture postcard. This popular means of communication was produced, sold, mailed and collected on a big scale. Everything new and interesting was pictured on cards by national and local producers. This included of course that pictorial new movement, the Boy Scouts. The fact that Scouting started in the last decade of what collectors call the 'Golden Age' of the picture postcard (1894-1918), made it possible to fill this book with pictures that otherwise would not have been made or had been lost.

After the first years Scouting developed into a world wide movement. Important events were the great Jamborees of 1920 and 1929, the start of an International Bureau in London and the invention of the Gilwell Woodbadge training for Scouters, with Gilwell Park as home base. In this book we follow the Scouts' trail up to the 5th World Jamboree of 1937 in Holland. For the 80-year-old Chief Scout Baden-Powell this was his last gathering with the movement he started thirty years earlier. For us this will be the moment to end our story, because on the cover we promised you to show 'old' picture postcards. Scouting, however, carried on and is still growing world wide. Today there are some 35 million Boy Scouts and Girl Guides in almost every country of the world.

Amongst the many millions of Scouts in the world only a small number are collecting. Most of them specialize in badges, and 'swopping' has become a popular Jamboree activity. Those who take the hobby more seriously join the International Badgers Club, founded in England in 1955. The IBC stimulates contacts the world over. In this club I met Peter Berry some fourty years ago. He rose to president of the IBC and I knew that he, apart from having one of the largest collections of badges, also had picked up a substantional number of early postcards. By mixing his collection with mine, I was able to compile the selection which illustrates this book. So the first person I have to thank is Peter, not only for offering me indispensable illustrations, but also for his additional comments, historical advice and general support.

To find the facts and figures I consulted the many books, magazines and newspapers on Scouting in my collection, which enabled me to include the original words used by the founder in his handbooks, the accounts of journalists present at the Jamborees, and the atmosphere laid down by contemporaries in official logbooks and souvenir albums.

The second person I have to thank is the publisher, a former Scout. Together, in Holland, we made a number of books on the history of Scouting, both national and international. The most successful one was 'De Padvinderij in oude ansichten' (Scouting in old picture postcards) which was published in 1975 and has been reprinted several times since. I hope this British equivalent will beat the Dutch record!

Last but not least, my thanks go to the staff of the Scout Association in London. Especially I would like to thank the archivist, Paul Moynihan, who helped me by checking facts and giving me invaluable advice. Scouting has a rich history, which is carefully preserved in the London archives. Historical material and souvenirs from the old days are always welcome. The address: The Scout Association, c.o. The Archivist, Baden-Powell House, Queen's Gate, London SW7 5JS. The Scout Association will benefit from a part of the profits of this book.

1 It was in the spring of the year 1908 that boys appeared in the streets of England, wearing broad-brimmed hats, coloured scarves knotted around their necks and armed with big wooden staves. Most amazing were their short trousers. The boys called themselves Boy Scouts and they were the first members of a movement that has grown ever since. This card, originally in colour, was published by the Inter-Art Co from London as part of their 'Artistique' series. Although the card dates from a few years later, this Tom Peddie portrait catches the atmosphere of the early days better than many a real photograph.

2 The new movement attracted many boys. In the meadows and fields around the cities and villages they could be seen practising observation, following trails and playing wide games. The least one could say about it was that this was a healthier environment than the big industrial cities with their narrow streets, smoking chimneys and no places to play. This photocard 'Im Ambush' comes from the well-known firm of Valentine's of Dundee. Their Boy Scouts Series dates from the first years, undoubtedly. Look at the brand new Scout hats and spotless new rucksacks of these boys. And they still have a lot to learn about stalking the enemy.

3 The boys even went camping in tents and tried to cook their own meals. The average Englishman didn't think much of the whole thing. Back in town these boys had to endure the cries of street gangs: 'Here come the Brussels sprouts, the stinking, blinking louts' and 'Go home, wash yer knees'! Until those days camping had been practised by soldiers and gipsies only. No wonder mothers were not instantly enthusiastic when their beloved son wanted to join the Scouts. Was the bed at home not comfortable enough and was there any reason to complain about mother's cooking?

The Scouts' Evening Meal—NOT as Mother makes it.

4 This is another card, made by Ernest Ibbetson, the well-known artist. Here he has drawn a more positive situation. The Scouts practise their daily good turns by sweeping snow from an old lady's doorway. Note the correct uniforms. In the early days most Boy Scouts did not wear a shirt, but a woollen jersey. The leather belt went over the jersey, the hatband was worn under the chin and the neckerchief was knotted around the neck. The shorts weren't as short as in later years. And the stockings, up to the knee, only showed a small part of bare leg. This card, as well as the previous one, was published by C.W. Faulkner & Co from London.

The Good Turn.

5 The best thing an early Boy Scout could imagine was a visit of General Baden-Powell. All Scouts from the whole town and the surrounding villages assembled in their best uniforms. This early post-card shows that the result was not yet very uniform. On Saturday, 18th January 1908, General Baden-Powell had explained his Boy Scout Scheme at a meeting in Birmingham with representatives of Y.M.C.A., Boys' Brigade, Church Lads' Brigade and others, interested in working among boys. Birmingham was one of the first big cities where Scout troops started. Not only within the existing youth organizations, but also by boys who formed patrols on their own accord.

INSPECTION OF BIRMINGHAM BOY SCOUTS BY GEN. BADEN-POWELL.

6 It's time to find out where this Boy Scout movement came from. This card brings us back in the year 1900. Colonel Baden-Powell had withstood the Boer siege at Mafeking for over seven months and had become a national hero. His portrait, with caracteristic Scout hat, could be seen on buttons, tea-cups, plates, cigarette cards and postcards like this one. A hundred years later Mafeking souvenirs still turn up at collectors' markets, antique shops and car boot sales. It gives an idea of the popularity of Baden-Powell and reveals how active manufacturers profited. Raphael Tuck & Sons did not take any chances. They expected Mafeking to be relieved any day, so they made three varieties of this card with the dates of 16th, 17th and 18th May. The right date proved to be the 17th, but the cards with the wrong dates were sold as well, to deal with the enormous demand for Baden-Powell cards.

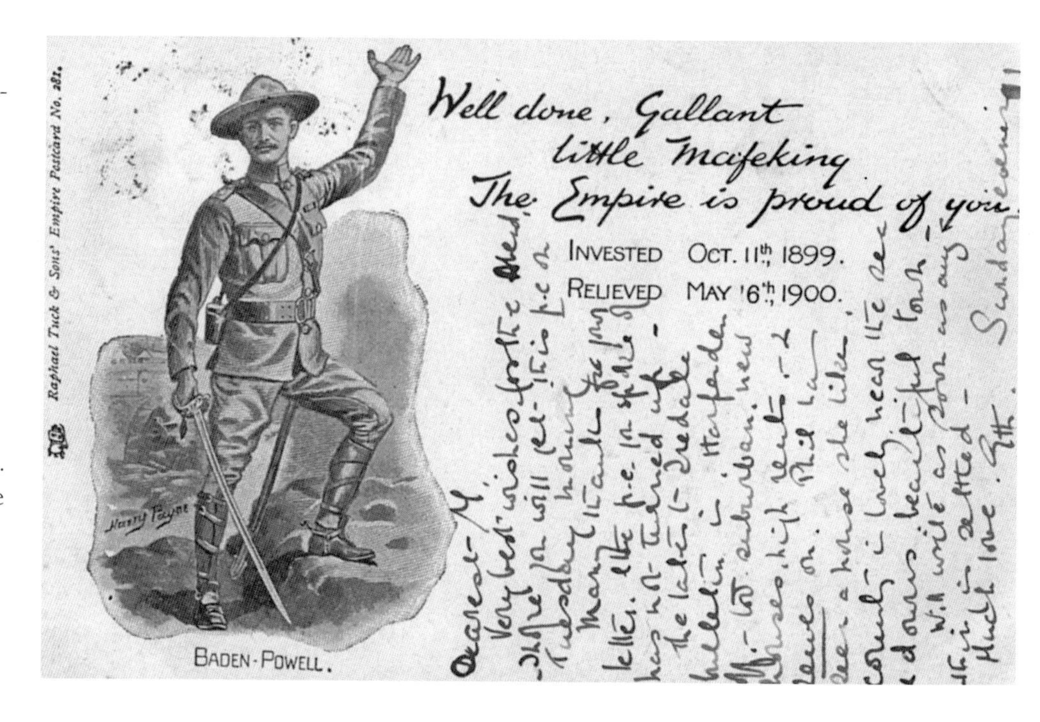

7 Queen Victoria promoted Baden-Powell. No wonder Major General Baden-Powell became a boys' hero overnight. He was the most romantic of all British officers. A pocketbook he wrote for his military Scouts became a bestseller amongst boys. It produced brilliant ideas to use when playing robbers or Indians. On his return to England in 1902, Baden-Powell found that it was used by school teachers and boys' clubs for their training in observation and deduction, leading to self-reliance, resourcefulness and good citizenship. Now and then he gave talks to Boys' Brigades and similar bodies and advised them to introduce a more romantic and less military program. This card dates from 1904, long before Scouting started.

8 To test his ideas for a better boys' program, B.-P. – as he affectionally was called – organized a camp for twenty boys on Brownsea Island in Poole Harbour near Bournemouth. On this privately owned and romantic location the boys practised all things a Scout should know and do: observation from trees, following trails, peaceful animal-hunting with a camera, sleeping in tents, lighting fires and cooking their own meals. For the boys it was a holiday nothing else could rival with. Think of the thrill to go and camp together with B.-P., the boys' hero himself! What an adventure for these lucky ones. The camp lasted for ten days and proved a big success. For this camp Baden-Powell selected boys from different ways of life. Some were sons of his friends, others were drawn from the Boys' Brigades of Poole and Bournemouth.

ON THE LOOK-OUT.
Lieut.-General Baden-Powell's Boy Scouts at Work and Play. No. 8.

PHOTOGRAPHING WILD CREATURES.
Lieut.-General Baden-Powell's Boy Scouts at Work and Play. No. 11.

9 The twenty boys were split up into four patrols, the Curlews, the Ravens, the Wolves and the Bulls. One of the boys acted as patrol leader. The patrols competed in all kinds of games. One of the most successful ones was harpooning the whale. Two patrols set out by boat from their own harbour, rowed to the spot where the (wooden) whale was sighted, harpooned the animal and towed it (together with the opposing boat probably) into their own harbour. The game showed the importance of teamwork. Another popular game was 'Bang the bear'. One big boy acted as the bear. He had three bases, in which he could take refuge and be safe. He carried a small air balloon on his back. The other boys were armed with clubs and tried to burst the bear's balloon while he was outside the base. The bear had a similar club, with which he tried to knock off the hunters' hats, which represented their lives. This was a good game for introducing strange or shy boys to each other, B.-P. wrote afterwards.

HARPOONING THE WHALE.

Lieut.-General Baden-Powell's Boy Scouts at Work and Play. No. 10.

PLAYING "BANG THE BEAR."

Lieut. General Baden-Powell's Boy Scouts at Work and Play. No. 9.

10 These drawings of the camp, made by Ernest Ibbetson, show boys in Scout uniforms, but that was beside the truth. The real situation, as seen on this photograph, shows that the clothing revealed the difference between the better-off boys and the boys from the back streets. The uniform introduced later took all differences away and proved to be a far more practical playkit than the temporary youth clothing. Note the broad-brimmed hats some boys are wearing. The patrol leader even has a Scout badge on its front. From the start helping other people was an important part of the Scout training. First aid to an insensible person was practised under the guidance of a Coastguard officer, who volunteered to help.

11 Here we see Baden-Powell leading the observation game 'Old Spotty-face'. A number of black paper discs have been pinned to a large sheet of cardboard, divided in squares. From a distance the boys have to try to find the right position of the dots and note this down on the miniature card they have at hand. Depending on the distance the player keeps and the number of rightly-noted dots, points are given. It is an excellent game for teaching long sight and fun to play too. Many games played at Brownsea Island Baden-Powell had borrowed from Ernest Thompson Seton, who had published these in his book 'Birchbark of the Woodcraft Indians'. On this photo we see that B.-P. does not wear his well-known Scout hat, but is experimenting with a small fold-up hat instead. Again we see that the boys are wearing civilian clothes, but some have a Scout badge on their arm. Remember this is August 1907. Scouting is still in the making.

12 After the Brownsea Island camp things went booming. B.-P. assembled the camp experiences together with many other ideas in a book he called 'Scouting for Boys'. Spread over six fortnightly volumes at fourpence each, it was within the reach of almost every boy. The volumes went on sale from January 1908 and they proved an immediate success. Publisher Arthur Pearson had arranged a tour of lectures by Baden-Powell in several big cities to pave the way for the book. The original idea of the founder was to introduce the game of Scouting to existing organizations like Boys' Brigade, Church Lads and Y.M.C.A., who adopted the ideas all right and organized troops. But completely independent boys also took on Scouting and started hundreds of patrols and troops themselves. The know-how from the book was enough to start a movement of its own.

Lieut.-General Baden-Powell's Boy Scouts at Work and Play. No. 6.

13 The year 1908 was a chaotic one. Everywhere Scouts appeared, improvising uniforms they had seen pictured in the book and playing games in public parks or fields, the nearest 'great outdoors' they could find. To help them on their way Baden-Powell issued postcards like this one, showing what uniforms should look like and how tents could be improvised by using Scout staffs as tent poles. The demand for the book was so big that publisher Pearson had to produce five reprints within the first year 1908. With the financial support of publisher Pearson Baden-Powell opened a headquarters' office, to deal with correspondence and supply equipment. He later told he remembered his secretary suggesting to have a stock of twelve Scout hats, would they be able to sell them all? The sale of the book made all scepticism needless. By the end of 1908 there were some 60,000 Scouts.

14 Camping in these early days cannot be compared to the way we do it now. There were no camping shops. Air-beds or fold-up-stretchers had not yet been invented. Weaving a camp mattress was the best thing a Scout could do to ensure a dry and soft night's sleep. Baden-Powell knew that during the night most cold comes from the ground. So he instructed his followers that a good mattress was of more importance than hiding under a big pile of blankets. The idea of a self-made mattress had been pictured in 'Scouting for Boys' and was tried out by Scouts immediately. In these days horses were still the main power for transport, so straw was easy to come by. One can imagine what the camping field looked like when camping equipment of this kind had been produced.

15 This card shows how the uniform should be worn. As from 18th April 1908 a new magazine was available for those wanting to be Scouts. Every week The Scout was filled with tips by Baden-Powell, information of the movement's growth and last but not least thrilling stories of adventure and good turns done by Scouts all over the British Isles. 'It is the simplest thing in the world to join the Boy Scouts,' B.-P. wrote in the magazine. 'I want every boy between ten and eighty to help his country by coming in touch with us. To become a Boy Scout you can: (1) Join a "patrol" or troop raised by any gentleman in your neighbourhood; (2) join the Boys' Brigade, or junior branch Y.M.C.A., who take Boy Scouts as part of their organization. If you are not a member of one of these, or if it does not as yet possess a patrol of Scouts, you can raise a patrol yourself by getting five other boys to join...'

16 'Scouting for Boys' was not a book to sit down with and read, but a source of inspiration urging the reader to form one of those patrols and go practise the games the author suggested. Harpooning the whale was a favourite, although it needed playing equipment that could not be found easily. That was not a new problem, however. In the summer of 1907 Mr. Henry Robson, the captain of the Bournemouth Boys' Brigade, received a list of what was needed for the camp from B.-P. Amongst things like tents, bedding, cooking gear and boats he found items that gave more difficulty to find. 'Harpoons, which Baden-Powell wired for on the eve of the camp,' Robson said later, 'were not readily obtainable in a small seaside town.' The Scouts on this photo seem to have solved the problems. They have boats and harpoons and also, one may trust, a life-like whale. This card was issued by Davidson Bros from London and sent to a Miss K. Jones with much love and XXX's from her 'Nursie'.

THE BOY SCOUTS. Harpooning the Whale.

17 At mischief before joining. Boy Scouts' good use of Holiday Hours. We doubt that the boys made their choice on these arguments but anyway, it's what parents and teachers could think of when Scouting came into question. This 'Tucks Post Card', number 9934 of the 'Oilette' series, was a coloured reproduction of a specially commissioned painting by Harry Payne, one of their most famous postcard artists. On the back the following information was printed: 'The Boy Scouts of Britain, initiated by Lieutenant-General Baden-Powell, number now over a quarter of a million, and are increasing every day. On holidays they roam the fields and woods in Scouting parties. Periodically they go into camp, and they are taught drilling, a strict code of honour, and civility. A famous preparation this, for their future duty of benefiting and defending their King, their country, and their homes!'

18 The daily good turn was one of Baden-Powell's most briljant inventions for the members of the young movement. All the different Scout Laws and the Scout Promise came together in this simple advice. On the back of these two cards can be read that they have been issued by the editor of The Scout, 'The Best Penny Weekly for Boys'. The clearly posed photographs give examples of situations each Scout could come across every day. Cutting firewood for a cottager or putting a stone under the wheel of a cart to give the horse a rest were good turns for which you did not have to search for long. The boy with the felling axe does not seem to be very well trained. The thing is too big for the job, is held in the wrong way and the branch he uses for a chopping-block is not steady enough to prevent an accident. Let's blame the photographer, who arranged the posing. The message of the picture, however, is clear.

CUTTING FIREWOOD FOR A COTTAGER. (Copyright)
Boy Scouts' Good Turns. No. 2.

PUTTING A STONE UNDER THE WHEEL OF A CART TO GIVE THE HORSE A REST. (Copyright)
Boy Scouts' Good Turns. No. 5.

19 Here we have two more cards in the Boy Scouts' Good Turn series. Two more ideas for noble activities: scattering sand in front of a cart on a slippery road and carrying a baby for a tired mother. The Scouts on these postcards were an example for boys all over Britain. They were members of the 1st Elstree, the troop of Scoutmaster Percy Everett. As manager of Pearson's he had visited the Brownsea Island camp and he had worked closely together with Baden-Powell ever since. Caught by the fever of Scouting, he started his own troop and so gained first-hand experience as a Scoutmaster. He became deputy Chief Scout eventually and was knighted for his services to his country through Scouting. In 1948 Sir Percy W Everett noted down his memories in the book 'The First Ten Years'. When he died four years later, Scouting lost one of its greatest and surely one of its longest serving friends.

(Copyright)
SCATTERING SAND IN FRONT OF A CART ON A SLIPPERY ROAD.
Boy Scouts' Good Turns. No. 4.

CARRYING A BABY FOR A TIRED MOTHER. (Copyright)
Boy Scouts' Good Turns. No. 6.

20 This is one of the best postcards in the world. Anyway, that's what J. Beagles & Co, E.C., printers and publishers, claim on the back of this card. It shows a good example of Scouting in the early days. We see a Scout, bringing a report after coming through the enemy's lines. Some Scoutmasters used their troop as a private army. Few things were regulated in the first years and there was much freedom for leaders to do as they pleased, even turning innocent boys into soldiers. The uniforms that 'Scout officers' designed for themselves in many cases included aigulets, spurs, swords, revolvers, gauntlets and riding-crops. Baden-Powell argued against all this, but from the beginning there were not, and never have been, enough Scoutmasters to deal with the masses of boys eager to be Scouts. Therefore it took some years before the Scouters' uniforms became more standardized.

21 This band on the march is pictured on another card made by J. Beagles & Co. from London. We see the same troop, this time ready to march off at the sounds of drums and bugles. On the big drum we can read ... North London. Under one of the cords the number of this troop is hidden. There are many signs to prove that it's an early photograph. Note the knotted scarves, the lack of badges, the sergeant's chevrons the boy with the dark shirt is wearing and of course the type of shoes, so typical of the early days. The Scoutmasters on the right have epaulettes on which the troopnumber has been embroidered. Anyway, that was a custom before nametapes were invented. The white shoulder-knot shows who is troop Scout-leader. And on the staff of a patrol-leader, somewhere in the rear, we see the flag with the animal after which the patrol has been named.

22 This is the type of uniform Baden-Powell wanted the Scoutmasters to wear. No military nonsense. Just Scouting decorations to show the boys that the grand man himself was not too old or important to wear the boys' dress. He even has proficiency badges on his sleeve. We recognize Ambulance, Seaman, Marksman, Fireman, Master-at-Arms, Signaller and Naturalist. Around the neck we see the green and yellow ribbon of the Silver Wolf. In the early days this decoration was awarded to Scouts who had gained at least twenty-four proficiency badges. Later on it became an honorary award and Scouters were advised to leave the wearing of proficiency badges to boys. B.-P.'s belt surely is one of the first official Scout belts, with a two-piece buckle showing the Scout badge and the motto Be Prepared. Note also the wristwatch; a pocket-watch, specially enveloped in a leather cover.

GENERAL SIR ROBERT BADEN POWELL

23 During the first months of its existence the weekly magazine The Scout had organized a competition amongst their readers. Thirty boys were invited to join the camp General Baden-Powell was planning for the next summer. 'The most fascinating holiday ever offered,' boasted The Scout. All expenses would be paid, including fares and food. The 'only thing' to qualify was to bring in the largest number of subscribers to the magazine. A system of voting had been arranged and in every next magazine one could see how many votes the best salesmen had secured. On 15th August the race ended with F.D. Watson on first place (with 29,018 votes) and A.D. Lippitt as happy number 30 (with 6,431 votes). During the contest the names of some 700 different successful boys had been published and it can be figured out that the magazine secured some 100,000 new readers. Not bad for a four-month-old. Baden-Powell was not happy with the competition, but he took charge of the camp anyway. It was organized at Humshaugh in Northumberland and borrowed many ideas from the Brownsea Island camp one year earlier.

SALUTING THE UNION JACK—THE ACTUAL FLAG THAT FLEW OVER MAFEKING. (Copyright)
Boy Scouts at Lieut.-General Baden-Powell's Holiday Camp. No. 5.

24 This Scouts' War Dance is an activity typical of the early days. Baden-Powell had been impressed by the Zulu culture he had seen in Africa and he described the war dance in 'Scouting for Boys'. 'Scouts form up in one line with leader in front, each holding his staff in the right hand, and his left hand on the next man's shoulder. Leader sings the Ingonyama song. Scouts sing chorus, and advance to their front a few steps at a time, stamping in unison on the long notes. At the second time of singing they step backwards. At the third, they turn to the left, still holding each other's shoulders, and move around in a circle, repeating the chorus until they have completed the circle.' At intervals one Scout acted in the circle how he had tracked down an enemy or stalked an animal. The leader started the singing with: 'Eengonyâma Gonyâma.' and the Scouts followed with the chorus 'Invooboo Yaboh! Yaboh! Invooboo!', which meaned: 'He is a lion! Yes! he is better than that; he is a hippopotamus!'

THE SCOUTS' WAR DANCE. (Copyright)
Boy Scouts at Lieut.-General Baden-Powell's Holiday Camp. No. 2.

25 The Humshaugh camp, held during the summer holidays of 1908, was carried out, as at Brownsea, on patrol lines. Someone present at this camp wrote: 'Perhaps the feature of the camp most looked forward to is the evening camp fire. A score of boys make their way into the wood and ply their axes with such good effect that soon a huge pile of wood is placed upon a convenient spot and a light put to it... The General, always an interesting personality, is perhaps seen at his best at these times. I can see him now with his hands clasping his staff as he answers the many questions put to him by admiring youngsters. "What star is that, sir?" says a curly-headed boy of twelve. "Is that the cry of the curlew?" enquires another. Be sure every question is answered, and the General proves himself to be an encyclopaedia of general information, and is as much at home with astronomy and natural history as he is with Scouting...'

ROUND THE CAMP FIRE—GENERAL BADEN-POWELL TELLS A SCOUT YARN. (Copyright)
Boy Scouts at Lieut.-General Baden-Powell's Holiday Camp. No. 6.

26 At the campfire Baden-Powell told about his adventures in India and Africa. A thrilling story about let's say following tracks or reconnoitring without being seen made the boys enthusiastic to try and do it themselves. That's what we see here on the last card from the 1908 Humshaugh camp. How many Scouts are there? It's difficult to find out, even while one of the patrol leaders fails to put his staff with patrolflag down. 'War Scouts and hunters stalking game always carry out two important things when they don't want to be seen,' Baden-Powell wrote in 'Scouting for Boys'. 'One is – they take care that the ground behind them, or trees, or buildings, etc., are of the same colour as their clothes. And the other is – if any enemy or a deer is seen looking for them they remain perfectly still without moving so long as he is there... In making use of hills as lookout places be careful not to show yourself on the top of the sky-line...'

AN AMBUSH IN THE PINE WOODS—HOW MANY SCOUTS ARE THERE? (Copyright)
Boy Scouts at Lieut.-General Baden-Powell's Holiday Camp. No. 1.

27 In the summer of 1909 this poster could be seen in London and elswhere. It invited the public to come to Crystal Palace and see for themselves what those Scouts looked like, the boys they had heard of so much in the past 18 months. The same poster invited Scouts to be present there: 'Boy Scouts in uniform admitted free.' The central picture was intriguing. A Boy Scout slid down a rope and had something in his arms, probably a child he had rescued from a house-on-fire. Together with the other promising activities like aquatic sports, music by military bands and grand spectacular displays there was reason galore to come to the palace in big numbers. The object of the gathering, as stated in the Headquarters Gazette was 'to demonstrate to the public the aims and the progress of the Movement and its stupendous growth since its initiation in the summer of 1907'. Nobody knew how many Scouts would be present and how they would behave. It was sure that many thousands of boys had been active as Scouts, but they all did it in their own way and the differences between the troops and patrols were gigantic. Was it wise to organize a happening like this, not knowing what the outcome would be and what the public might think having seen it?

28 Perhaps it's best to listen to Baden-Powell, how he described the meeting thirty years later for BBC-radio: 'In that year, 1909, I arranged to have a meeting of the would-be Scouts at the Crystal Palace on a certain day. And when I got there, my wig, there were a lot of them. Rain was threatening, so we mustered them inside the Palace and arranged a March Past and counted them as they entered at one door and went out at the other. And there were 11,000 of them – 11,000, who had taken it up of their own accord! That is why I say one didn't see the start: Scouting just started itself...' A program was drawn up of competition in bridge-building, tent-pitching, signalling, life-saving, camp-craft, cooking, ambulance, drill, and other Scout subjects. These competitions had been worked out in the districts and the final heats took place before an enthusiastic public.

29 One of the things that made this rally go down in history as very important, was the presence of Girl Scouts. One of the brave forerunners of the Girl Guides is pictured on this card. The girls had borrowed hats from Scouts who were unable to go to the rally themselves, and were eager to get a place in the new movement. In history it is often said that it surprised B.-P. when he came face to face with these girls at the rally, but in reality he was well aware of their existence and had written about this in The Scout. He had received letters from girls long before this day, one reading: 'Dear Sir, If a girl is not allowed to run, or even to hurry, to swim, ride a bike, or raise her arms above her head, can she become a Scout? Hoping that you will reply. Yours sincerely.' Earlier, in 'Boy Scouts Scheme', published in 1907, B.-P. wrote: '...To ladies interested in the care and education of girls, I think this scheme might supply a suggestion for an attractive organization and valuable training...' The girls caught the attention they wanted and not long afterwards a separate movement for Girl Guides was formed by Agnes Baden-Powell, the sister of the founder.

THE BOY SCOUTS. A Girl Scout Comrade.

30 Here we see the Scout badge. Baden-Powell gave the following description in the first edition of 'Scouting for Boys'. 'It's the arrowhead, which shows the north on a map or on the compass. It is the badge of the Scout in the Army, because he shows the way: so, too, a peace Scout shows the way in doing his duty and helping others. The motto on it is the Scout's motto of BE PREPARED. (B.P., my initials), which means that a Scout must always be prepared at any moment to do his duty, and to face danger to help his fellow-men. It's scroll (not pictured here) is turned up at the ends like a Scout's mouth, because he does his duty with a smile and willingly. The knot is to remind the Scout to do a good turn to someone daily. A Scout's badge represents and is called his "life". It is given him when he passes the tests in Scout-craft necessary to make him a Scout.' The three parts remind the wearer of the Scout Promise and the points of the two stars stand for the ten Scout Laws.

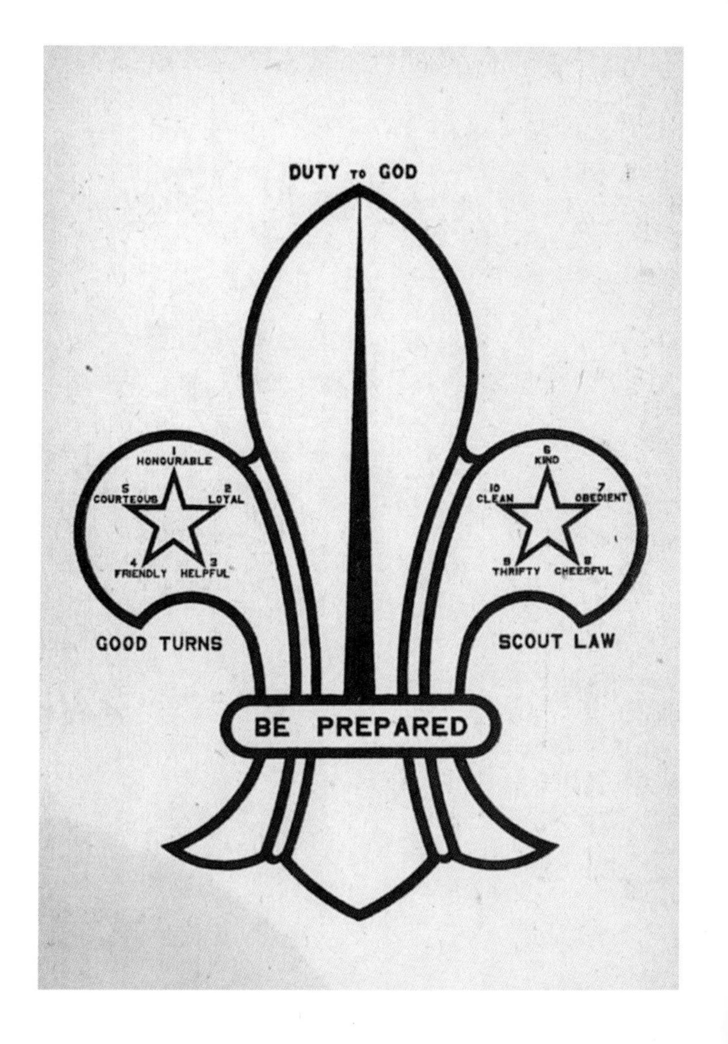

31 This card from the Welsh Folk Museum shows a 1908 certificate given to Arthur Short after his enrollment as a Boy Scout. Certainly a treasure a Scout would hang by his bedside as a reminder of his promise made and showing all the things that a Scout could do and gain: camping, stalking, life-saving, all the knots, proficiency badges, patrol flags, utensils for games and sports, leaves and fruits of nature, the complete Scout badge, the Union Jack and the Chief Scout himself. Scouting stands on four pillars: Outdoor-life (camping, stalking, etc.), Patrol System (working in small groups under a self-chosen boy-leader), Scout Law and Promise (concentrated in the instruction to 'do a good turn daily'), and Learning-by-doing (no theory, but immediately trying things out, preferably in the form of a game). Add to that the romantic uniform with colourful badges, and it's clear why so many boys were eager Scouts.

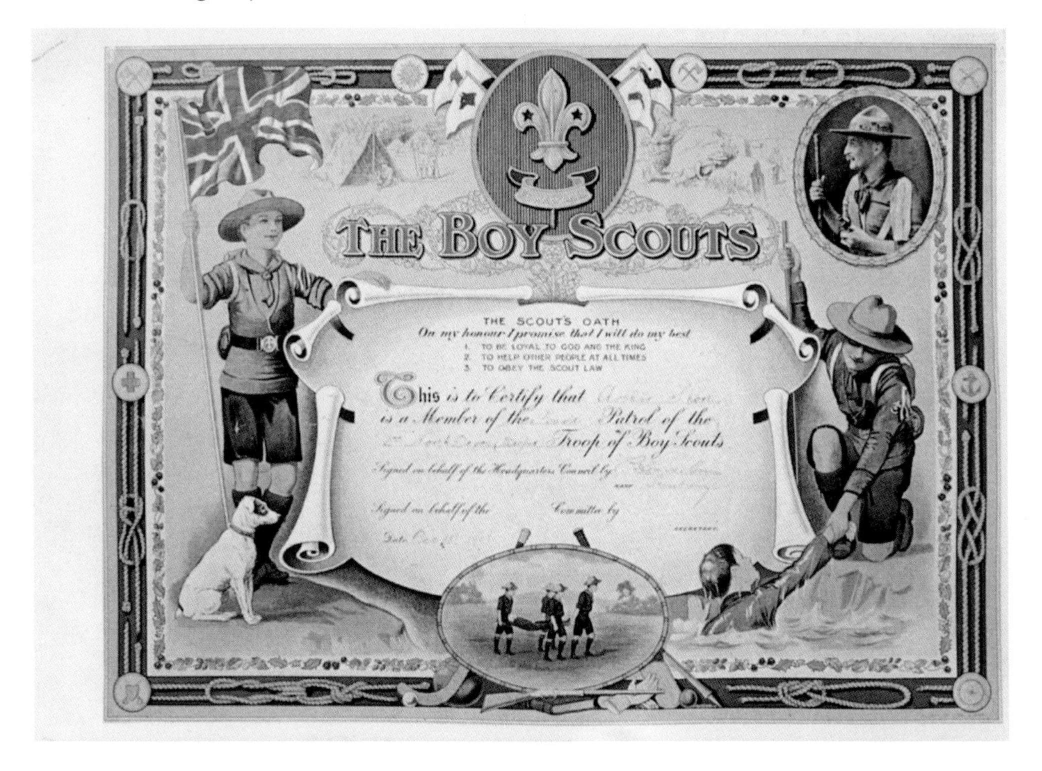

THE BOY SCOUTS

THE SCOUT'S OATH
On my honour I promise that I will do my best
1. TO BE LOYAL TO GOD AND THE KING
2. TO HELP OTHER PEOPLE AT ALL TIMES
3. TO OBEY THE SCOUT LAW

This is to Certify that
is a Member of the Patrol of the
Troop of Boy Scouts

Signed on behalf of the Headquarters Council by

Signed on behalf of the Committee by

Date

32 Badges formed an important part of the system. A trained Scout was a man of many trades. He was an experienced camper and showed this in gaining the proficiency badges for Camper, Naturalist, Prospector, Stalker, Weatherman and Woodman. His self-dependence was shown in the badges for Athlete, Cook, Engineer and Healthy Man. To prevent boys to go into factories as an untrained worker, Baden-Powell stimulated boys to get badges as Basket Worker, Blacksmith, Carpenter, Electrician, Leather Worker, Plumber, etc. The local professionals were often the examiners and many a time they found a good apprentice in the young Scout, worth giving a job for life. To promote the working for badges, these special awards were in use. Once a boy had become a First Class Scout, he could progress through further tests to become a King's Scout. These tests included earning four Service badges such as Fireman, Interpreter, Handyman or Swimmer. A Scout who earned 24 badges and performed a service to the Boy Scout Association could gain the Silver Wolf, which was worn around the neck on a green and gold ribbon.

33 These two cards, from a series published by R. Johnson & Sons LTD from Manchester, show medals for gallantry and good service. The Cross for Saving Life was available in two grades: the highest, the Bronze Cross with a red ribbon, could only be won where the claimant had shown special heroism or had faced extraordinary risks. The Silver Cross with a blue ribbon stood for gallantry with considerable risk. The Medal of Merit was meant for those who did duty exceptionally well in cases of emergency, though without risk to themselves. On this early card the inscription on the cross reads 'For Saving Life'. Later on this was changed to 'For Gallantry'. In 1917 a Gilt Cross (red and blue ribbon) was introduced as the third stage and the Medal of Merit became an award for both boys and officers who performed service to the Association. After 1921 it was only awarded to officers. The medals were worn on the right breast.

34 This drawing by Dudley Buxton on a C.W. Faulkner card gives a nice impression of an early Boy Scout 'dining out with a regimental friend'. Scouting was no military movement, of course, but the uniform, the custom to give troops a number, the use of words like Scout officer and corporal, and the fact that the whole thing was an idea of a well-known General, did not help to convince the public that Baden-Powell's peace Scouts were no soldier-playing kids. B.-P. was aware of this risk and tried everything to change these ideas, but this was not always easy. At the Crystal Palace Rally, for instance, well-wishers of the movement presented prizes for the various competitions. One of these, a field gun, presented by Sir H. Mackworth Praed to the troop which was adjudged the smartest in appearance and drill, became a useful weapen, figuratively, to anti-militarists. The joke on this card, however, referring to the military, did not have the intention to harm the movement. How different were those days without a McDonald's on every street corner!

35 All Patrols Look Out, is the slogan on this card, number 8 in the 'Humourous' series, issued by James Brown & Son, Official Boy Scout Publishers in Glasgow. In June 1909 Rudyard Kipling had devoted a song to the Boy Scouts.
'These are our regulations – There's just one law for the Scout. And the first and the last, and the present and the past, And the future and the perfect is "Look out!"... Look out, when you start for the day, That your kit is packed to your mind; There is no use going away With half of it left behind. Look out that your laces are tight, And your boots are easy and stout, Or you'll end with a blister at night. (Chorus) All Patrols look out!...' The song continues to tell what to look out for. The birds in the air, ditches hidden in the innocent knee-high grass and many other things under the sun. Mr. Kipling became a friend of Scouting and in later years got especially connected with the junior branch, the Wolf Cubs.

36 'Every British boy should study the Navy as much as possible, and learn the history of the different ships,' wrote Baden-Powell in 'Scouting for Boys'. 'Perhaps you may like to know some facts about the dress of the sailors,' he continued and explained the origin and benefit of the flap collar on their back, that the three white lines commemorated Nelson's naval victories – The Nile, Copenhagen and Trafalgar – that the black silk tie was a mark of mourning for Nelson's death, and that their baggy trousers made it easy to roll them up when they wanted to wade. Boys like that sort of information. In the summer of 1909 The Scout ran another voting contest and gave 100 boys a chance to attend a camp with Baden-Powell. The big party was split up in two. One half boarded the training ship Mercury, the others camped at Buckler's Hard, and halfway the parties changed places. This camp is considered to mark the start of Sea Scouting.

An Appreciative Audience.

37 The place for this Sea Scout camp was again something special. The trial camp of 1907 had been on a romantic island. The second, in 1908, near Hadrians Wall in the North. This time two historic scenes were chosen: the land-party camped on the natural slipway where Nelson's ships had been built. The others stayed at the Mercury, owned by the famous cricketer C.B. Fry. The boys learned all kinds of things sailors should know. The making of knots and splices and the use of sextant and compass, as shown on this card, surely will have been part of the program. The uniforms of the boys at the 1909 camp looked different from the ones we see here. This card is from years later. In those early days most Scouts stuck to the kaki uniform with in some cases only a different hat. Instead of the broad-brimmed hat a sailor cap was used.

38 In 1912 the Sea Scout branch got its own handbook 'Sea Scouting and Seamanship for Boys', written by W Baden-Powell K.C. and issued by James Brown & Son of Glasgow. The Chief Scout's older brother Warington had been in the Merchant Navy and B.-P. liked to tell how in their youth Warington took his brothers George, Frank, Stephe and Baden on extensive cruises along the coasts of Scotland and England on his yacht the Diamond in all seasons of the year. 'From the educational point of view,' the Chief wrote in 'Lessons from the Varsity of Life' (1933), 'the discipline, the endurance of hardships and the facing of danger involved in this cruising, were points of lasting value in one's training for life.'
Many Sea Scout troops were well equiped, as we can see on these cards, issued by the Boy Scouts Association in 1925.

Sea Scouts, Launching a Whaler. (1148)

Sea Scouts, Picking up a Tow. (1144)

39 'The object of the Sea Scouts is to teach lads at or near the sea seamanship, navigation, pilotage, knotting and splicing, how to handle boats under oars and sail and a number of other duties which appertain to the life of a seaman,' Admiral Charles Beresford wrote in the foreword to the 'Sea Scouting for Boys'. He added: 'They should also all learn to swim, not only to be able to save themselves, but to save the lives of others in the event of an accident.' Many Sea Scout troops practised life-saving regularly and became very efficient at it. This was in line with the Scouts' Motto 'Be Prepared', train beforehand, be alert and act as experts when needed. The know-how of life-saving had spectacular sides. At shows for the general public Sea Scouts fired rockets with life-lines from the coast to ships in danger and rescued the passengers.

Sea Scouts, Sail-making and Flag repairing (1143A)

Sea Scouts, Practice with Life-saving Apparatus (1150)

40 A headquarters is a great help for any troop. This Sea Scout H.Q. is, as this postcard shows, usable for many purposes: the storage of smaller boats, oars, sails and masts, the practising of knotting, rigging, sports, etc. In some cases the headquarters was built in the form of a ship. The 'Land-Ship Scouter' built by the Sea Scouts of Rose Hill School, Tunbridge Wells, was famous in that respect. But something artificial remained attached to it. The year 1937 proved to be a red-letter year for Sea Scouts with the acquisition of that old gallant ship, the R.R.S. Discovery, which was their established headquarters for many years in the heart of London river.

41 Sea Scouts have their boats; Scouts ashore have their own means of transport. In the old days trek carts were important. Just think of the heavy material tents were made of then. No lightweight cloth, no aluminium tent-poles, no plastic groundsheet, no metal pegs. Everything was made to last and a patrol that wanted to make a hike couldn't do without a good trek cart. With the arrival of the new cart a new game became possible: racing with trek carts. Competition between patrols was organized to find out who was quickest in taking the cart over a high obstacle. This photograph, taken in July 1910, shows how the cart is taken apart in pieces that are passed over the fence. Once the cart has been completed and the camping gear has followed and been loaded, the end of the race probably is putting up the tent and hoisting a flag to show that the team has finished.

42 This troop has several types of trek carts avaible, one for water, the other for all sorts of transportation. When you compare the size of these wheels with the ones used in the obstacle race, it becomes clear that these are the 'Rolls Royces' of trek carts. Manufacturers advertised trek carts in The Scout and elswhere, fitted with 'artillery wheels and best steel springs'. They claimed that their carts could be dismantled and assembled in a few seconds (!). Of course every Scout in the patrol helped moving the thing. Look how the ropes on the wheels will help to get the load over all kinds of hights and how the large wheels make it possible to keep going even on the most difficult ground.

No. 6. A SCOUT'S WATER CART

No. 4. TREK CART DRAWN BY CYCLISTS.

43 These cards show that even a river or stream does not stop the patrol. After finding a good spot, spars are lashed together and one Scout is manoeuvred to the other side of the water. Now it's possible to start making a bridge or just heaving all goods and personnel across. Trek carts were made in a huge number of sizes and with all sorts of options, including means to hang, when not in use, lamps, galvanized swivel-hook guide ropes, fold-down sides, painted in troop colour and with troop number and even 'regulation large ruby back-light'. Some of these early trek carts have survived the many years of service and are treasured by the Scouts of today. Now and then trek cart races are held again. Just for the fun of it and also as a salute to the Scouts of years gone by, pictured on these postcards.

44 This postcard takes us back to 1910, to the 1st Bollington, Cheshire, Company of Girl Guides. It's visitors' day at the camp and one can imagine what the mothers in their Edwardian dresses think of the modern ideas of their daughters. Sleeping in tents and roving the countryside with big hats, Scout staffs and rucksacks. In the Handbook for Girl Guides, Miss Baden-Powell wrote: 'We go into camp not only because we enjoy it so much, but also to gain experience. A Girl Guide likes to try her hand at making things, and finding out how to do a thing herself in a way she can't do at home. Some people talk of "roughing it" in camp, but these people are generally "tenderfoots". A wise Guide does not "rough it"; she knows how to look after herself, and to make herself comfortable by a hundred little dodges. The best place to my mind for a camp is in or close by a wood where you have leave to cut firewood and to build huts. Bell tents can be hired in almost any town for a few shillings per week, or you can buy a second-hand one in good condition for about £2.'

45 The Girl Guides Association was officially formed in 1910, but the movement had already been moving for almost two years, when girls started reading 'Scouting for Boys' and got down to business immediately, claiming 'Anything boys can do we can do better'. Uniforms had been improvised in a wide variety and it was difficult to get all girls, their determined leading ladies included, moving in one direction. Founder Baden-Powell had his hands full in getting the boys' movement off the ground and some people feared that promoting Scouting for girls could have a bad effect on a boy's interest to join the Scouts. B.-P. asked his sister Agnes to take the lead and he himself did everything to stimulate Guiding. First of all, together with his sister, he wrote the handbook 'How Girls can Help to Build up the Empire'. And secondly he welcomed Guides at local Scout rallies. This photo shows how the General inspects a Guide Company at the Brighton rally in February 1910.

46 This patrol of Scottish Scouts welcomes us to their camp with the new Boy Scout Salute. In 'Scouting for Boys' Baden-Powell had described the Scout's Salute and Secret Sign. When a boy was invested and took the Scout's Oath, he was 'holding his right hand raised level with his shoulder, palm to the front, thumb resting on the nail of the little finger, and the other three fingers upright, pointing upwards. This is the Scout's salute and secret sign. When the hand is raised shoulder high it is called the "Full Salute".' Together with the Scout staff, this led to complications, and therefore in 1911 a new salute was introduced, made with the left hand while the Scout staff was held by the right hand. This postcard, issued by C.W. Faulkner en Co. Ltd. from London, brings us to the biggest and most representative gathering of Scouts in the early days. The date was 4th July 1911, a day of blazing sunshine, the place was Windsor Great Park. On the next pages more pictures from that historical rally can be seen.

C. W. Faulkner & Co., Ltd "Daily Mirror" Photograph.

KING'S REVIEW OF BOY SCOUTS.
The new Boy Scout Salute.

47 In Headquarters Gazette, the magazine for Scout officers, the rally was vividly described by Marcus Woodward. Quoting his account not only provides us with original details, but also shows how proud the Scouts were at and after this extraordinary happening. 'The great day of the Royal Rally, the greatest in the history of the Boy Scout Movement – its Coronation Day, one might say – is to be written down a magnificent success. July 4th 1911, will never be forgotten by anyone then so happy to be in Windsor Great Park. The Boy Scouts have taken home with them a memory, the story of which, we may be sure, will lose nothing in the telling when their grandchildren are about them in ages to come...'
The Daily Mirror Photographs on these two cards show how the Scouts – there were some 30,000 of them present – took up their positions and how the King's Scouts, who were to play an important part in the show, arrived at the Rally Ground.

48 King Edward VII was very interested in the Boy Scouts and had agreed to Baden-Powell's suggestion that boys who passed special tests for proficiency should be ranked as King's Scouts. And B.-P. in turn agreed to the King's suggestion that he should bring his Scouts to Windsor, some time in 1910, for a royal review. The death of the King in early 1910 changed the plans for only one year. King George V asked the Scouts to stage the promised rally as soon as they could and so the 4th of July was chosen, a fortnight after his Coronation on 22th June 1911. On the eve of the rally Baden-Powell wrote to the King: 'There will be between thirty and forty thousand Scouts on parade out of our 200,000. These have all passed some tests in tracking, cooking, first-aid, ambulance, missioner, signalling, field telegraph, pioneering, and other such work. Numerous cases have occurred of public work being performed by Scouts in aid of police or in accidents, notably last week in the Coronation accident at Barnstaple, and in the arrest of an armed murderer at Red Deer, Alberta.'

C. W. Faulkner & Co., Ltd. "Daily Mirror" Photograph.

KING'S REVIEW OF BOY SCOUTS.
Patrol Leaders and Scout Masters receiving final instructions.

C. W. Faulkner & Co., Ltd. "Daily Mirror" Photograph.

KING'S REVIEW OF BOY SCOUTS.
Ambulance Display.

49 'The Scouts present include 100 from Canada, detachments from Malta, Gibraltar, Ireland, Scotland, and Wales, as well as from all parts of England,' Baden-Powell continued in his letter to King George. 'All Scouts wearing medals have saved life. Of these there are 229. King's Scouts wear a crown on the left arm; of these there are 2,397. Badges on the left arm stand for tests passed in various handicrafts. Of these 137,000 have been issued. A cord around the shoulder means that the wearer holds at least six efficiency badges. A silver wolf around the neck means at least twenty-four proficiency badges have been gained...' The King's desire for information about the Scouts, especially to enable him to recognize badges and distinctions of honour, can be understood from what is between the lines of this letter. When on the right place for the inspection, the Scouts rested on the grass, but when B.-P. passed for a last minute inspection of the thousands, they jumped up and held their hats on their staves in a cheering salute.

C. W. Faulkner & Co., Ltd. "Daily Mirror" Photograph.

KING'S REVIEW OF BOY SCOUTS.
Resting before being inspected by the King.

C. W. Faulkner & Co., Ltd. "Daily Mirror" Photograph.

KING'S REVIEW OF BOY SCOUTS.
Boys cheering Lieut.-Gen. Sir Robert S. S. Baden-Powell.

50 The big moment drew near. A royal carriage with a pair of greys drove up with little Prince George, who came in for an ovation. Then came four greys, and the Queen, bowing to the Scouts, the Prince of Wales, Princess Mary and Princess Christian with her. Then came the King's cavalcade: Life Guards, a line of Indians in gorgeous uniforms, the King, smiling and saluting, with Baden-Powell to his side, followed by the Duke of Connaught, General Prince Christian, Major Prince Alexander of Teck, and the trim, little, much worshipped figure of Lord Roberts among others. It took the royal party clear fifty minutes to pass the two- or three-miles-long row of Scouts. On the postcard can be seen that they stood ten rows deep. Funny detail: the small Scout on the 6th row seems to be more interested in the newspaper-photographer who, one can imagine, under a black cloth and behind his large camera, is acting like a magician.

51 The finale of the rally was a very special one. The King took his place under the Royal Standard at the saluting point. Baden-Powell on his fine black horse, the gift of some New Zealand admirers, sounded his whistle for the most stirring incident of the day – the Grand Rush, invented for the occasion. A sudden roar filled the air, and the whole mighty horseshoe of thirty thousand boys lept forward from either side, rushing as only boys can rush, gathering speed and force as they came, screaming out the rallying cries of their patrols. It sounded like the zoos of the world having been let loose. The thirty thousand closed in on the King as a great foaming wave, and it seemed that nothing would stop them. Spectators trembled lest the King should be enveloped. But at a line, which none but the Scouts knew, the wave stopped dead, as if suddenly frozen. The shouting and the tumult died, and then – silence. A line of banner bearers advanced and marched past in what King George considered the prettiest picture of the day, followed by gallant life-savers. The end was a cheer which lasted for ten minutes, while a forest of Scout hats on staves shot up.

C. W. Faulkner & Co., Ltd. "Daily Mirror" Photograph.

KING'S REVIEW OF BOY SCOUTS.
Cheering the King.

52 We leave the British Isles for a while to see how Scouting has spread on the Continent and elswhere in the world. This early card comes from France. Scouting crossed the Channel quickly. In 1908 Nicolas Benoit, a lieutenant in the French Navy, founded the 'Fédération des Eclaireurs de France'. He had to make some changes to make Scouting acceptable to his countrymen. The fleur-de-lis was a symbol with a political meaning and therefore he took as symbols the Gallic rooster and a bow-and-arrow. The Eclaireurs were an association open to everyone. In successive years associations for Protestant, Roman Catholic and Jewish Scouts were founded.

53 This card, originaly in bright colours, shows us a Swiss Scout or Eclaireur. Switzerland is divided into 23 counties or cantons. In some of these Scouts had started and in 1912 a national association was formed. On this card, mailed to England in 1914, we see that the Swiss Eclaireur wears the familiar Scout uniform. The badge, however, is different from the British one and follows the style of the French Eclaireurs. The preference for a crossbow was in honour of William Tell, the national hero, who with this weapon shot an apple from his son's head. In later years the Swiss changed to an arrowhead-badge too, in the national colours red and white.

54 Scouting had started in Austria in 1910. The Wiener Pfadfinder-Korps, active in the Austrian capital, issued this postcard. The previous cards, from France and Switzerland, showed the familiar types of tents that were also used by the British Boy Scouts. This photograph from the summer camp at Neulengbach proves that the Austrian Scouts utilize a mixture of canvas tent and wooden hut. They call it a Zelthütte, a tent-hut, and it's a type that has been used by Scouts from Austria, Czechoslovakia and neighbouring countries for many years afterwards.

55 Scouting was exported to Holland by a patrol of six Boy Scouts of the 16th Oxford troop. In the summer of 1910 they cycled to Hull, took the ferry to Rotterdam and during a three-week tour they visited uniformed youth organizations in Rotterdam, Amsterdam and Tilburg. Their photograph was published on the front cover of Holland's most popular weekly and this made their visit a national event. Thanks to this tour Scouting was started that same year and this card here shows the first Amsterdam troop in early 1911. There is something special about their outfit. When Baden-Powell visited Holland in August 1911, he met these Scouts and wrote about them in his book 'Boy Scouts beyond the Seas': 'One thing which these Amsterdam Scouts did especially well was throwing the lasso. They all carried light cord-lasso's on them. These came in useful for hundreds of things, like making bridges, rope-ladders, rescuing people from burning houses, and so on. But the Scouts also used them for lassoing each other, and many of them were awfully good at it.'

56 In The Hague Baden-Powell met another Scout movement. They didn't copy English Scouting, but had developed a Dutch variety with a lion as symbol and badge. B.-P. was amazed by their demonstration of first aid. In The Scout he wrote: 'The Dutch Scouts had an excellent stretcher, which I think would be very useful for some of our ambulance patrols. With its help, one Scout alone could take an injured man to hospital.' The fact was that the Scouts in The Hague were trained by a medic who had invented and developed material for the Medical Corps of the Dutch Army. The account in The Scout was accompanied by sketches Baden-Powell had made of the stretcher, including how it could be hung under a patrol car. That enabled one Scout to wheel the patient to the hospital. In 1911 Scouting started in no less than 40 Dutch cities. The self-dependent troops differed quite a lot, but after a few years they all joined together in one national association.

57 In 1910 Baden-Powell had payed a short visit to the United States, but in early 1912 he had more time available to see how Scouting had flourished there. The story how Scouting had come to the USA, is a classic in Scout history. Mr. Boyce, an American newspaper man, got lost in the London fog and was rescued by a Boy Scout performing a good turn by bringing him to the address of his appointment. Impressed that the boy refused a tip, Boyce took the idea to the States. From the beginning American Scouting was well organized. The National Headquarters in New York stimulated a good financial background by linking every troop to a sponsoring body, the use of a uniform uniform, provided by an official outfitter, and an excellent Handbook for Boys, kept cheap by lots of advertisements. These early cards show the uniforms and the easy-to-carry shelters, much lighter than the traditional Bell-tents, especially for hiking on foot or by bicycle.

"Sending Semaphore Signals."

Photo by H. H. Simmons, St. Louis, Mo.

"Instruction in Knot-Tying."

58 From the beginning the Boy Scouts of America had their own style. First of all there were the traditions and skills of the pioneers. Famous men like naturalist Ernest Thompson Seton and backwoodsman Dan Beard took the lead in the program and throwing a rope was a natural part of that. On the other hand the most modern techniques had been adopted. The use of a wireless station was more than playing a game. Many a time Scouts saved lives with these contacts beyond the horizon. Baden-Powell met Scouts in all the big cities: 1,000 paraded in Boston, 500 in Washington, where B.-P. was received by president Taft. In Detroit he met American and Canadian Scouts, in Chicago 5,000 Boy Scouts awaited him and in New York no less than 4,000 and among these a troop of Chinese Scouts. Other cities and rallies followed. He travelled on to Canada, Japan, China, Australia, New Zealand and South Africa. Everywhere he was welcomed by Scouts. The movement surely had a firm footing now all over the globe.

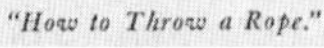

59 Let's go back to old Europe. Here we see that Scouting also had found its way to Germany. These members of the Deutscher Pfadfinderbund practise signalling with a flag. When you compare this early postcard with some a few pages back, you realize that there were many different signalling systems in use. In these days many countries had their own-invented system, used by their army and the less another country could understand it, the safer and better it was. These Germans, however, probably use the Morse-system and by doing that they're ahead of their time. Germany was divided up into several countries with their own King or Prince, their own stamps and, of course, their own Scout movement. The dress of these Scouts from Munich recalls the outfit of the German colonial army. The ideals, no doubt, were the same as elsewhere: they came from the book 'Pfadfinder', 'Scouting for Boys' translated into German.

Deutscher Pfadfinderbund

60 Helping other people and life-saving in particular were favourite activities of Boy Scouts everywhere. Society was not as well organized as today and so there were chances galore for good turns. Traffic with automobiles was something new and many an old lady was happy with the Scout who helped her across the street. Dealing with accidents fell to the people who happened to be on the spot. But the most attractive job was that of firefighter. Scouts have helped in many ways. Scarfs turned into smoke-masks, lassos into life-lines, staffs and coats into stretchers. This troop from Belgium is specializing in this kind of work. When the alarm is sounded, the fire engine, hoses and ladder will be at the site of calamity in no time. And you can be sure that the firemen-on-foot, who stand behind the engine, will follow in full speed.

61 Boys are the same everywhere. This happy crowd was photographed in Spain. The Exploradores de España from Zaragoza have their summer camp at Ordesa. The spirits in this Scout camp seem high. In the center of the photograph we see the chaplain and he also had a central place in the life of the troop. On the Continent it took some time for the conservative Roman Catholic Church to discover the benefits of Scouting. Only in the twenties and thirties they accepted this form of youth work, but from then on Scouting grew spectacularly in Roman Catholic circles, not only in Spain, but in France, Belgium, Italy, Holland and many other countries also. This priest had the vision earlier, because this card is from before the First World War. Scouting started in Spain in 1912 and the King was an active member of the movement. Fifty Spanish Scouts were present at the Jamboree in London in 1920.

62 Going around to all countries where Scouts were active from the early days, would take more room than this book provides. As last of the series of foreign postcards we take you to Scandinavia. There they were quick to accept Scouting. In Denmark and Sweden the movement started in 1909 and in Norway and Finland in 1910. This postcard shows us Danish Girl Guides or Pigespejdere in Frederiksberg Gardens. The first girls on the Scouting track joined boys' troops (as happened in many other countries) and after a number of years they got their own national association.

63 After our tour around the world we return to England. That's exactly what Baden-Powell did in 1912. On his journey he had not only found Scouts everywhere. On the boat to America (January 1912) he met a young lady by the name of Olave Soames and the two married on October 30th that same year. They spent their honeymoon camping in North Africa and the Chief Scout could happily report to the Scouts 'Olave is a perfect wonder in camp – thoroughly enjoys the life and is as good as a backwoodsman at it.' Almost a hundred thousand Scouts contributed a penny each for a wedding present. When it arrived, this photograph was made to show the Scouts their gratitude. The car was a 20 h.p. Standard, painted green (the Scout colour) and later on it was adorned with a Scout statuette on the radiator.

64 Let's go back to the simple Scout life and leave motor cars behind. This postcard shows the highlight of every Scout's camp, whether at a big international gathering, the camp of a troop or with just one patrol. We have many cards in our collection with this kind of view. Something to put in a frame and hang on the wall. Albert Stiebel & Co. from London made this easy. They printed the frame on the card. There's one special technique that most of these cards have in common, a trick that might be forgotten in these modern times. It can be recognized by the facts that the fire gives an exceptionally good light and that there's one Scout sitting between the fire and the camera. The trick is that this fellow has a small packet of magnesium powder in his hand. The lens of the camera is opened. The Scout throws the powder in the fire, making sure the movement is invisible. And the fire acts as a modern flash-light. What do you think of the result?

65 When on Bank Holiday August 1914 the First World War broke out, most of the Boy Scouts were in camp. Mobilization was a matter of a few minutes, and the work which they were now called upon to perform had, in many places, already been practised in the form of a Scouting game. Baden-Powell issued instructions regarding the non-military work which Scouts might undertake: guarding and patrolling bridges, culverts and telegraph lines against damage by spies; collecting information as to supplies and transport avaible; handing out notices to inhabitants, and acting as dispatch riders, signallers, etc.; helping families of soldiers; establishing first-aid stations, refuges and/or soup-kitchens in their clubrooms; and acting as guides, orderlies, etc. With their ability to rig their own shelters, to cook their own food and to regulate their own roster of duties in their patrols, the Scouts were already organized in the best practical units for such duties.

66 An abbreviated form of the Chief Scout's instructions had previously been communicated by telegram to the County Commissioners and Secretaries, who had immediately put the services of the Scouts at the disposal of the authorities. The civil and military authorities on their part lost no time in making use of such services. It was the rapidity of the Scouts' mobilization which astonished everyone. Before the Territorials could be mobilized – within the first hours after the outbreak of war – Boy Scouts were out guarding telephone wires and railway bridges, and they carried out their self-imposed task until men became available.

Feeling that they were taken seriously, the Scouts acted with much enthusiasm. Too much here and there, probably. The designer of this Raphael Tuck card gives a humorous example of this. Two tiny Scouts have taken prisoner a German band in military-looking uniforms. If this ever occurred, the matter will have been cleared in peace, we trust. The public looked upon the eagerness of the boys with pleasure.

67 Goodwill for the Boy Scouts can also be sensed from these two comic cards. The kids were not wanted to handle guns, of course, but guarding the coast was a job that was not only carried out during the first hours of the war. At the request of Lord Kitchener, detachments of Sea Scouts were sent to help the Coastguard at their duty of watching for and reporting enemy warships. When the men of the Coastguard were called away to join the Fleet the Scouts took over their coast-watching duties, and there they remained, carrying on the work under the orders of the Admiralty at every station from John o' Groats in Scotland to Land's End in Cornwall and the system was later extended to cover naval bases, wireless and air stations. Between 5th August 1914 and 7th March 1920 (when they were demobilized) about 32,000 Scouts altogether passed through the coast-watching service, the number actually on duty at the same time being between 1,500 and 2,000.

68 'On the outbreak of war the Boy Scouts volunteered to provide a batallion for the Front, which, however, was not needed. Nevertheless, most of the older Scouts, together with their Scout-masters, went off and joined His Majesty's Service, Navy and Army – some 40,000 of them – and splendid work they have done, earning among them several Victoria Crosses and other decorations, as well as commissions as officers,' Baden-Powell reported after the war. 'You might think that with so many leaving to take up service, the corps would cease to exist – but it didn't; on the contrary, there are many more Scouts in it now than there were when the War began. Many thousands of Boy Scouts won the coveted little strip of red with yellow date upon it which you will see them wearing upon the right breast. It is the badge of having done War service of one kind or another.' This card shows a scene of the patriotic film 'Wake Up!', produced and distributed by the Daily Express.

69 The Welcome Sound, produced by a Boy Scout, more than any other war service, made the movement popular with the inhabitants of London and of other places. Remember that attack from the air was something new in warfare. During the air raids of 1917-1918 Germans in huge silent Zeppelins and other enemy aircraft flew over a city and dropped bombs at any spot, be it of military importance or not. Scouts always have been good at improvising and in a situation like this their bugles proved to be more valuable than anyone could have imagined a few years earlier. The boys on duty, day and night, blew 'Take Cover' to arouse Londoners from their sleep and to send them to their cellar steps. When some time later the sky was clear again, the 'All Clear' was sounded, which brought about general relief and made the bringer of the good news the most popular kid on the block. The work the Boy Scouts did during the war got publicity on the Continent through 'The War Pictorial', a colourful magazine, printed and published by The Illustrated London News and Sketch Ltd. There was a continental edition in French and Dutch and in 1918 four of the monthly magazines made the good work of Boy Scouts and Girl Guides known abroad.

70 This card was sold in aid of the Boy Scouts' Motor Ambulance Fund. By their own efforts, the Scouts supplied and staffed seven motor ambulances for the soldiers in France. A number of Scouts were on hospital duty in France with the Society of Friends' Ambulance. Colonel H.S. Roche, R.A.M.C., wrote to Scout Headquarters in 1916: 'I should like to take this opportunity of telling you what excellent work the Boy Scouts car and its team did in the troublous times round Ypres in April and May when it took its full share of the trying and dangerous work of getting the wounded away every night under considerable shell-fire. Sergeant Hodson himself is one of the most energetic, resourceful and helpful N.C.O.'s out here. If he is a typical product of the Boy Scout training, your organization has done much for the future of the nation.'

71 Another job the Scouts carried out was the setting up and running of four recreation huts for the soldiers in France. There were several clubs in Britain as well, and this card here is the front of the membership card for the Soldier and Sailor Scouts' Club at 68 Victoria Street in London. B.-P. has sketched in his inimitable way the help provided by the Boy Scouts to the fighting men, carrying the kitbag and rifle for the successful soldier, who, in his right hand, holds a symbolic trophy: the helmet of a defeated German enemy. The most famous Scout hut was the one at Etaples, France, where the Chief Scout himself, together with his wife, joined the staff to give the soldiers a friendly welcome behind the lines. Baden-Powell's frequent trips to France caused rumours that he was active as a spy. The publication of his book 'My adventures as a Spy' in 1915 will have played a role in this. This, however, was not more than a rumour as the Chief had too much other work at hand, of which you will read more on pages to come.

72 Active and former Boy Scouts could be found everywhere in the Army and the Navy. In the Battle Cruiser Fleet gatherings of Old Scouts were organized. Just before the Battle of Jutland one of such meetings brought together 230 Old Scouts. 80 of them went under in the Jutland Battle. One of them was the 16-year-old Boy 1st Class John Travers Cornwell, V.C. He was wounded early in the action, but nevertheless remained alone at his most exposed post, quietly awaiting orders. In the Scout movement it was decided to keep alive the little South London boy's memory by means of a fund which was to provide scholarships and grants for starting promising Boy Scouts in their professions. During the war some thirty Scouts qualified for such scholarships and grants, but in many cases the Fund was not called upon to provide them, since many Scouts, after serving in the forces, made their own way to successful careers. Jack's memory also lived on in the 'Cornwell Scout' badge, an exceptional award in respect of pre-eminently high character and devotion to duty, together with great courage, endurance and gallantry. This exclusive decoration, often awarded to physically handicapped Scouts, was nicknamed the Scout's Victoria Cross.

THE GREAT BOY SCOUT.

73 During the First World War some 40,000 Scouts and Scoutmasters joined His Majesty's Army and Navy. Thanks to their Scout training many of them performed above average and the splendid work they did was honoured by eleven Victoria Crosses and many other awards and distinctions, as well as commissions as officers. On the outbreak of war Baden-Powell had offered to provide a batallion of Scouts for the front, but this offer was not accepted and old- as well as active Scouts could be found in all parts of the armed forces. This card honours one of the many members of the movement that didn't come back. Roland Philipps, a Scout since 1911 and Commissioner for East London, had bought a house in Stepney Green as a centre of Scouting for the slum area. Having written classic books like 'The Patrol System', he was one of the well-known Scouters of the early years. When he was killed at Olivers in 1916, only 26 years of age, the Chief voiced the feeling of the movement when he wrote that 'part of the soul of Scouting had gone'. This card, issued by the French Scouts, shows Philipp's grave at Aveluy Village Cemetery, near Albert.

74 In 1916 'The Wolf Cub's Handbook' was published, marking the start of a new young branch of the movement. Up to this time the boys from eight to eleven years old had either been excluded altogether from the joys of Scouting or had been admitted, under age and against the rules, to Scout troops, thereby tending to make the Scouts feel themselves ridiculous. This photograph shows a young boy acting as a mascot for the troop. He seems proud enough with this task, and the smiles on the faces suggest that the troop enjoys the fun. The Chief Scout recognized that the needs of young boys were different from those of the elder ones and the Cub training was designed on lines quite separate from those of the Scouts, yet complementary to it.

75 The Cub, like the Scout, was given a Law and a Promise, a uniform and badges, but these were quite distinct from those offered to his big brother the Boy Scout proper. Baden-Powell had been busy thinking over and planning a program for junior Scouts for several years. The start of the war had caused a delay, but the demand for this new branch was big. He asked Miss Vera Barclay, up till then a successful Scoutmaster, to try out the ideas he had so far with a bunch of little Cockneys as guinea-pigs. He handed over to her, what she later called, a lovely hotch-potch of papers, mostly notes in his well-known handwriting and the rest in clippings and little pen-and-ink drawings. Hers was the job to straighten these into a new handbook, and to think up badges and tests.

These two cards show Cubs from the first years. This can be recognized by the knotted scarves and the antique type of shoes. Note the variety of stockings: there had been no standard type or colour until those days.

Wolf Cubs - just started on the Scout Trail.

76 Central theme of the new Wolf Cub branch was the story of Mowgli, told by Rudyard Kipling in his Jungle Books. The writer and Nobel-prize winner Kipling was one of England's favourite writers and poets and the Jungle Books, issued in 1894-1895, were bestsellers in his extensive oeuvre. This card shows the opening ceremony of the meeting: Akela, the leading wolf, is in the centre of the circle of Wolf Cubs. At her side is the sixer (the Cubs' equivalent of patrol leader) who is in charge of the totem of the pack. The Cubs howl: 'Akeela, we'll do our best!' The ceremony appealed strongly to the boys because it was a mixture of running and shouting, it payed attention to the Wolf Cub Law and was a clear mark that the 'official' meeting had been started. Kipling generously gave permission to use his ideas, because he was a supporter of Scouting. His son John took part in the Sea Scout camp at Bucklers Hart in 1909 and in the same year Kipling wrote the 'Patrol Song' for the movement. At the time of Cubbing's start the Kiplings and the Baden-Powells were almost neighbours, living at Ewhurst Place and Burwash in Sussex respectively.

77 The Wolf Cubs received their own Law, as pictured on this official card, issued by the Boy Scouts Association. The Cub leaves his play to help other people and withstands the temptation of cookies on the table. The Law was much shorter than that of the Scouts, but difficult enough for a young boy to live up to.
The Wolf Cub's Handbook, divided in 'Bites' was an instant success and the first edition sold out within a very short time of its appearance. The movement, launched in a period when many might have predicted failure for any new enterprise not directly connected with winning the war, met with phenomenal success, and proved useful in supplying the small boy with a legitimate method of letting off steam at a time when, in the absence of so many grown-up influences, he might have drifted towards hooliganism or so-called 'juvenile crime'.

THE CUB LAW.
(A) The Cub gives into the old Wolf.
(B) The Cub does not give into himself.

78 This is not just a pack of Wolf Cubs but (as the writing on the back of this card reveals) the winners of the 'Wimbledon Association Challenge Shield', which is proudly shown by the sixer next to Akela. The year is 1924 and Cubbing has stabilized since the first hectic years. There are a few things to look at. The yellow Cub flag on the left. The caracteristic totem at the right, with the wolf's head and the honours won by the Cubs in the form of (often leather) ribbons. The Cub officer is in dress uniform with, on the front of his Scout hat, the green badge of rank. Many of the Cubs have stars on their caps, awarded for general training. These were called their 'eyes'. When a wolf-cub is born his eyes are not yet open. By training in all things a good Cub should know, a first and a second star were awarded. Three-angled proficiency badges on the right arm stand for achievements in character, handicraft, physical health and service to others.

79 This is no doubt the world's best-known Cub Scout: Peter Baden-Powell, the son of the founder. Peter was born in 1913 and this card will be from around 1920. The age for a boy to join the Cub Scouts was eight years, but Peter had some special introductions to enable him to wear the green cap and jersey earlier than that. At special occasions he accompanied his father and he must have felt uncertain at times. There's a photo in the official Jamboree Book 1920, showing the Duke of Connaught, accompanied by the Princesses Mary and Louise, and many other important people and, tiny amongst all the chic dresses and bright uniforms, were the 'Chief Cub' Peter, six years old at the time and the 'Chief Brownie' Heather, just five and barely able to see anything from under her straw brownie-hat. The life of a crown prince is not always easy, but on this card the Chief Cub is smiling anyway. Many of his colleagues will have been jealous. They saw the Old Wolf himself only now and then from a distance.

80 The Boy Scouts Imperial Headquarters at 25 Buckingham Palace Road, London SW1, was for many decades the heart of the movement in England and the goal of a pilgrimage for many foreign Scouts. The building was opened in 1917 by the Duke of Connaught who on this great occasion was presented by B.-P. with a very special award: the only Gold Wolf in existence. The growth of the movement obliged to try and find a new and more spacious building and at '25 B.P. road' this was found. Note the big badges hanging from the front of the building, and the windows of the Scout Shop, cramped with all kinds of merchandise that made a member of the movement's mouth water. At the age of eighty Chief Scout Baden-Powell spoke about the old days for BBC-radio and remembered his '... secretary suggesting that if we laid in a stock of 12 Scout hats, would we be able to sell them all?' Since then things had boomed. Let's enter the building and have a look at what started with that dozen of broad-brimmed hats.

81 Welcome in the Scout Shop. The assistants are waiting to serve you. Some 75 years later every collector of Scout memorabilia sees things on this card he or she would die for to possess. First of all there are the many books, written by the Chief Scout and other authors. The colourful reproductions of paintings, ready framed, from famous painters like Ernest Carlos. A recent photograph of the Chief Scout or the Prince of Wales. Cub Scout posters, drawn by B.-P. with space to print your own text, trophy-shields, postcards, stationary, and all the other things helpful to play the game. Note the practical suitcase in the centre, next to the patrol leader/shop assistant. This is especially made to carry a commissioner's uniform, the brim of the hat protected against getting curved. If you want a uniform or camp equipment, the assistants will go and get these for you from the stores behind the curtain. This is not self-service, you see. Here you get personal attention and expert advice.

82 On the first floor of the building there are the offices. In this room we find a meeting of the National Committee. We recognize some of the members, from left to right: the Earl of Meath, K.P., Boy Scout Commissioner for Ireland, the Chief Scout (Sir Robert Baden-Powell, also Commissioner for Training of Officers), unknown, P.B. Nevill, Esq., Commissioner for Kindred Societies, Major Lord Hampton, D.S.O., D.L., Chief Commissioner, P.W. Everett, Esq., M.A., F.S.S., Chief Scout's Commisioner and Commissioner for Equipment, unknown, and H.S. Martin, Esq., C.B.E., International Commissioner.

A COMMITTEE

83 Elsewhere in the building at 25 Buckingham Palace Road we find the general office and the packing department. The office deals with the registration of troops, the issuing of warrants to leaders, the distribution of badges, the editing of The Scout (every week) and The Scouter, formerly the Headquarters Gazette, (every month), and all the other things needed to keep a big movement like Scouting on the move. There are a number of young Scouts active in the office. They work in uniform (of course!) and the job at IHQ is practical training which helps them on their way to make a living as a clerk. At the packing department the orders of customers are prepared for transport. The Scout Shop had customers not only on the British Isles, but all over the world. Many foreign Scout associations ordered their badges from London and especially the troops in other parts of the British Empire wanted genuine uniforms and badges to show their link with the ones who invented the great game.

GENERAL OFFICE

PACKING DEPARTMENT

84 The London headquarters building is prepared for all situations, just like a Scout should be. Here we see the Club Smoking Room and the Club Dining Room, where employees as well as visitors are welcome. These and the previous four views of Imperial Headquarters come from a booklet with twelve tear-out picture postcards, issued by The Commercial & General Photographic Co. of Marloes Road, Kensington, in 1923. Almost the only thing IHQ did not provide for was sleeping accommodation. In 'The Scouter' however the Rubens Hotel offered its services to London visitors. 'One minute from Victoria Station. Most convenient for H.Q. meetings, Imperial Headquarters being actually in Hotel Building...' When in 1961 Baden-Powell House was opened in South Kensington, the Scout Association had its own hostel and when in 1974 Headquarters moved to a new building next door to B.-P. House, staying overnight in London again could easily be combined with a H.Q.-meeting. The Scout Shop, now operating under the name Camping and Outdoor Centre, still has a branch on Buckingham Palace Road.

THE CLUB SMOKING ROOM

CLUB DINING ROOM

85 In 1919 an important step in the development of Scouting was the institution of a scheme of training for officers in the movement. Yet in 1914 the Chief had published a 'Scoutmasters Training Course' combined with practical experiments in London and other districts on the lines suggested. The war had interfered, but in 1919 plans could be continued. In that year Mr. W.F. de Bois Maclaren, Commissioner for Rosneath, Dumbartonshire, paved the way. He bought for the Boy Scouts Association the Gilwell Park estate of fifty-five acres of land, including a manor-house, on the borders of Epping Forest. The object of the gift was twofold: a training centre for Scouters and a camping site, especially for less experienced troops and for poorer Scouts. The house on this card developed to become the Mecca of Scouting. From here came the power that still keeps the engine of International Scouting running.

86 Gilwell Park became a hit overnight, especially with the Scouts from East London, who could be found on its fields the whole year round. Away from the crowded city and yet not too far to reach walking, with camping-gear loaded on the patrol trek cart. This postcard takes us back to a sunny day in the early years. It's not one of the many posed-for photographs, made to illustrate official books, but a view of what Gilwell was really like for the young Scouts. It's too hot for shirts, stockings and shoes. There's a tree to climb, fresh air to breathe and sunshine to get a tan. Look at the fashionable white pants of the gentleman near the tree, the long shorts the boys wear, the Bell tent in the background. This must be in the twenties. More proof wanted? The small text on the card mentions Gillwell Park; written with four L's. That's how the name was spelled till 1929. Then Baden-Powell added Gilwell to his name, on becoming a Lord. Old papers revealed then that the most accurate spelling was Gilwell with three L's.

87 Another view of busy Gilwell Park. Like the previous card this one was published in the Farringdon Series. The Bathing Pool. Here was a good chance to try out what Baden-Powell had suggested in 'Scouting for Boys'. 'No Scout can be of real use till he can swim,' and learning to swim is not more difficult than learning how to ride a bike. All you have to do in the first place is 'to try and swim like a dog, as if trying to crawl slowly along in the water; don't try all at once to swim with the ordinary breast stroke that swimmers use, because this only lets your mouth go under water every time. When paddling along like a dog get a friend to support you at first with a pole or his hand under your belly.' The Scout Law is the rule of the camp. It's not written down anywhere, but the Laws are observed nonetheless and not the least important of them is 'Be Clean'.

THE BATHING POOL GILLWELL PARK. Farringdon Series

88 This postcard brings us back to 1919. Gilwell was officially opened on Saturday, 25th July, in perfect weather. The Chief Scout and his Lady were present to receive guests at tea. The Hall was formally opened by Mr. and Mrs. Maclaren in the presence of some 700 Scouts. The first regular training course was held from 8th to 19th September and was attended by some twenty Scoutmasters from all parts of England and Wales, and of vastly different ages and professions. The Chief Scout marked the event by blowing the historic Kudu-horn, brought from Matabeleland in 1896 and used at the Brownsea Island Camp in 1907. The photo reveals some remarkable facts. The leather thong on the brim of the hat shows a number of wooden beads. These came from Dinizulu's necklace, a souvenir from the 1896 Matabele Campaign. Two beads on a thong were to be the 'Wood Badge', awarded to Scouters completing their training. Not to wear on their hat, as originally planned, but around the neck on the Gilwell neckerchief (with Maclaren tartan patch on the point) and held by a leather woggle (a brand new novelty that was gladly adopted as part of the uniform by Scouts all over the world).

89 The men attending a course sank their identities and became, for purposes of training, Boy Scouts in the 1st Gilwell Park Troop. The Troop was divided into three or four Patrols, each man taking his turn at being Patrol Leader, Second, lowest Scout, etc., for a day in rotation. The work carried out consisted of lessons in Troop organization, campcraft, pioneering, woodcraft, signalling, games, fieldwork, pathfinding and a study circle. The program was directed by the Camp Chief, who was assisted by his Deputies. Francis Gidney was the first Camp Chief. He was an imaginative leader with wide experience in Scouting. 'He brought a touch of controlled lunacy to the place,' an early helper recalled. His campfires would be enlivened by ax- and knife-throwing but the fundamentals of the training remained those laid down by Baden-Powell in his in 1919 published book 'Aids to Scoutmastership'. The fame of the Gilwell Training soon spread through the international movement and branches sprang up all over Britain, the Commonwealth and in foreign countries.

90 Gilwell Park Camp Chief Francis Gidney had to learn the Scouters to train their boys through games. He was a perfect 'boy-man' with a boyish sense of humour and great enthusiasm to try out new things. When we keep this in mind and add the fact that he was in his twenties, it's understandable that he did not always follow the same tracks as the office people at Headquarters in London, who were twice his age. He left Gilwell in 1923 and was succeeded by John (Belge) Wilson, a former police officer, who carried on the training into the Second World War, and became director of the Boy Scouts International Bureau afterwards. Gidney's spirit lived on and his name is attached to the training for ever, also through the Gidney Log Cabin we see on this card. It was built in 1929 as a memorial to the first Camp Chief in the north-east corner of the park.

91 The Chief Scout loved to be at Gilwell. He liked to pop in occasionally to see how the training was progressing, giving a spontaneous lecture if suitable and having a stimulating word for everyone. Here we see him in the middle of a number of Scouters, listening eagerly. Every year at the end of August a Gilwell Reunion was organized. Those who had attended the practical training or been made a 'Gilwellian' earlier, came together for a weekend of social contacts, picking up new ideas and gathering fuel for the coming Scout year. Gilwell Reunions are held to this day and now these are gatherings with Scouters from all over the world, all gone by the same training and recognizable by their Gilwell scarf and wood badge. For most of them this is a first visit to the 'holy grounds' they only know from photographs and tall stories. The Gilwell Training worldwide is the engine that keeps Scouting running the way the founder meant it. The engine has been developed through the years, but still runs on the basis taught at Gilwell Park.

Chief Scout at the Council Fire. FARRINGDON SERIES.

92 There is a song, known all over the world, the chorus of which goes: 'In my dreams I'm going back to Gilwell, to the joys and the happiness I found. To those grand weekends with my dear old friends, and see the Training ground. Oh the grass is greener back in Gilwell, and I breathe again that Scouting air, while in memory, I see B.-P., who never will be far from there.' This card shows that dream. Here is B.-P. surrounded by boy campers, who perhaps meet their idol for the first time face to face. Baden-Powell frequently stayed at this Gilwell Park, the heart of Scouting, for several days. In the early twenties he hung his hammock somewhere to spend the night in. From 1929 he had his Eccles caravan, presented to him by the Scouts, parked at Gilwell permanently. This photograph, published by J. Farringdon, has been reissued by Gilwell Park recently, the picture faded out into an oval form, like a dream and only with 'Gilwell Park in the early days' written on the back. Not everyone will recognize the Chief on that photo. Surely he will never be far from there.

93 It is Saturday, 31st July 1920. In Olympia Hall, London, the Boy Scouts' International Jamboree takes place. This first ever World Jamboree was quite different from the ones held nowadays. It was more or less a big circus where the general public could see what Scouting really was. Baden-Powell's subjects, laid down in the program, were 'to stimulate energy among the Troops, to make aims and methods better understood, to recruit Scoutmasters, to bring Overseas and Foreign Scouts into closer touch and to push forward our organization in the densely populated industrial centres where moral and physical training is so badly needed for the boys.' The moment pictured here is the 'Grand Howl', performed by five hundred Cub Scouts. Akela Vera Barclay, who organized this act, travelling in the Underground, overheard one businessman say to another: 'The little chaps doing their Grand Howl is the best thing in that show.' Not only the public was won by the giant green pack; foreign Scouts took the idea home and from that day Cub Scouting became popular worldwide.

94 The Scout's Camp was situated in the Old Deer Park, Richmond, and housed 6,000 under canvas. The place was in easy travelling distance from Olympia. The competitors and performers of the show took possession of the many Bell tents and there were marquees to be used as camp offices and for recreation, chapel, hospital and catering uses. Here also the rehearsals for the show took place. These included trek cart work, fire-fighting, tumbling, Morris dancing, physical training, gymnastics, ambulance work, bridge-building, camp-pitching, signalling, wrestling and musical drill. Special displays included country life and industries, collierly life, life of Saint Patrick, the Red Hand of Ulster, a Highland gathering, the life of the Chevalier, customs of the Arawak Indians and African native life. A pageant written by B.-P. called 'The Genesis of Scouting' told the story of Captain John Smith in Virginia and of Princess Pocahontas.

95 Two more pictures from the canvas city in Richmond Old Deer Park. With almost no public around, this was an ideal location for foreign Scouts to meet one another. The British Commonwealth was well represented with contingents from Australia, New Zealand, India and South Africa, and deputations from Ceylon, Gibraltar, Jamaica, Malaya and Malta. From abroad almost all European countries had sent contingents, but there were also large or smaller deputations from America, Chile, China, Japan and Siam. The South African contingent, pictured here, numbered 186 Scouts. 'The boys from the Transvaal wore a distinctive strip of Leopard Skin round their hats and the rest a Gold Springbok Head sewn on the shirt,' wrote the 'World Jamboree Book', issued afterwards. Special badges were rare in those days and the one mentioned here, the first World Jamboree contingent badge, now is a much wanted piece of Scout memorabilia. The Sea Scouts had prepared a very spectacular show. From the artificial rocks in Olympia Hall they fired rockets with life-lines to the antique ship and hoisted castaways to safety.

96 'At the close of the great Jamboree at Olympia on Saturday night Boy Scouts, representing twenty-six nations, acclaimed Sir Robert Baden-Powell Chief Scout of the World. Well did he deserve it, for through him a great gift has come to the boys of Great Britain, and from them has spread it to the boys of all nations,' The Times wrote on 9th August. 'If only we could seize the "microcossus Jamborensis" and inoculate the whole world with it, there would be better hope of the immediate present and of the immediate future. The Boy Scout is one of the best hopes of the world. More power to their poles! There are still foul dragons which await their slaying,' commented The Daily Telegraph on 2nd August. The sight of that international concourse of boys marching together, so soon after the war, moved many to tears. The general feeling after the Jamboree was pictured by Punch in the famous style of the popular magazine. This card went all over the world to testify to Scouting's success.

Reproduced by kind permission of the proprietors of "Punch.

WAR-WEARY WORLD *(at the Jamboree)*: "I was nearly losing hope, but the sight of all you boys gives it back to me."

LE MONDE, ÉREINTÉ PAR LA GUERRE *(au Jamboree)*: "Garçons, peu s'en fallut que je ne perdisse espoir, mais je la sens renaître à la vue de vous tous."

IL MONDO, SPOSSATO DALLA GUERRA *(alla Jamboree)*: "Perdivi quasi ogni speranza, ma la sento rinascere alla vista di voi tutti ragazzi."

EL MUNDO, ABRUMADO DE LA GUERRA *(a la Jamboree)*: "Yo estaba para perder esperanza, pero la vista de vosotros todos los muchachos me le ha restituida."

97 During the Jamboree two International Meetings of Scout leaders were held. It was decided that a regular conference should be held biennially, and that the next should be in Paris in 1922. It was also recommended that an International Bureau should be established in London. This was made immediately possible by the generous financial support of Mr. F.F. Peabody of the United States of America. His encouragement was further strengthened by another American, Mr. Mortimer Schiff. The administrative and driving force was provided by Mr. Hubert S. Martin, C.V.O., C.B.E., who for eighteen years served as the Honorary Director of the Boy Scouts International Bureau. He is seen on this photo, holding in his hand a copy of 'Jamboree', Symposium of Worldwide Scouting, issued in English and French four times a year.

98 A very special moment in the life of a Scout is his investiture ceremony, pictured on this card. The troop is lined up in a horseshoe formation, with the Scoutmaster and Assistant Scoutmaster in the gap. The Tenderfoot, in this case a Wolf Cub who has completed his first years in the movement and, being 11 or 12 years old now, has joined the troop. His Patrol Leader, who in the past weeks has helped him on the new track, stands behind him: a safe feeling. The Assistant Scoutmaster keeps the troop flag ready. The Scoutmaster asks: 'Do you know what your honour is?' and 'Do you know the Scout Law?' Then, making the half salute sign with his right hand, his left hand on the troop flag, the recruit repeats after the Scoutmaster: 'I promise on my honour, to do my duty to God and the King, to help other people at all times, to obey the Scout Law.' The Scoutmaster finishes the ceremony by saying: 'I trust you on your honour, to keep this promise. You are now one of the great brotherhood of Scouts.'

Investiture of a Tenderfoot Scout.

99 The cards on this and the following pages come from a series of ten cards, issued in the twenties. They give us the possibility to go back in time and see how the Scout Law was pictured in photographs that were representative of the time. We don't have space enough to show all ten cards, but have chosen the four we like most. We add what B.-P. told about them in 'Scouting for Boys'.

1. 'A Scout's honour is to be trusted.' If a Scout says 'On my honour it is so,' that means that it is so, just as if he had taken a most solemn oath. If a Scout were to break his honour by telling a lie or by not carrying out an order exactly when trusted on his honour to do so, he may be directed to hand over his Scout badge, and never to wear it again.

2. 'A Scout is loyal to the King, his country, his officers, his parents, his employers, or those under him.' He must stick to them through thick and thin against anyone who is their enemy or who even talks badly of them.

100 Scout Law 3: 'A Scout's duty is to be useful and to help others.'.And he is to do his duty before anything else, even though he gives up his own pleasure, or comfort, or safety to do it. He must be prepared at any time to save life, or to help injured persons. And he must try his best to do at least one good turn to somebody every day.
4. 'A Scout is a friend to all, and a brother to every other Scout, no matter to what social class the other belongs.' Thus if a Scout meets another Scout, even though a stranger to him, he must speak to him, and help him in any way that he can. A Scout must never be a Snob. A Scout accepts the other man as he finds him, and makes the best of him. The cards in this series not only have been sent around among Scouts, showing them the Scout way. They also were used as an example for a series of cigarette cards, issued by Ogdens in 1929. It proves that these free premium-cards were well documented before the designer made the drawing, in colour, because these postcards, made by the Boy Scouts Association, showed the official views of the movement.

101 Scout Law 5: 'A Scout is Courteous.' That is, he is polite to all – but especially to women and children, and old people and invalids, cripples, etc. And he must not take any reward for being helpful or courteous.
6. 'A Scout is a friend to animals.' He should save them as far as possible from pain, and should not kill any animal unnecessarily, for it is one of God's creatures. Killing an animal for food or an animal which is harmful is allowable.
7. 'A Scout obeys orders of his parents, patrol leader, or Scoutmaster without question.' Even if he gets an order he does not like he must do as soldiers and sailors do, and as he would do for his Captain in a football team, he must carry it out all the same because it is his duty.
A notable thing of the Scout Law (and the advice Baden-Powell added, which we quote here) is that it's not negative by telling what's forbidden, but positive by enumerating what a boy should do.

Scout Law 8: 'A Scout smiles and whistles under all difficulties.'. When he gets an order he should obey it cheerily and readily, not in a slow, hang-dog sort of way. Scouts never grouse at hardships, nor whine at each other nor swear when put out, but go on whistling and smiling. The punishment for swearing or using bad language is for each offence a mug of cold water to be poured down the offender's sleeve by the other Scouts.

9. 'A Scout is thrifty,' that is, he saves every penny he can, and puts it into the bank, so that he may have money to keep himself when out of work, and thus not make himself a burden to others; or that he may have money to give away to others when they need it.

10. 'A Scout is clean in thought, word and deed,' that is, he looks down upon a silly youth who talks dirt. A Scout is pure and clean-minded and manly.

It's many years since the Chief Scout wrote down these words in 'Scouting for Boys'. The photos look 75 years old. What about the ideals behind the ten Scout Laws?

A Scout Smiles and Whistles under all Difficulties. (1124)

103 Baden-Powell was a man of many trades. He was not only a famous soldier, a journalist (he wrote for many newspapers), a writer (with over forty books to his name), an illustrator (he sold sketches to The Graphic and illustrated his own writings), and a painter (his watercolours were beautiful), but also a gifted sculptor. This card shows a statuette of St. George, the Patron of the Boy Scouts. The text on the back of this card says: 'With best wishes for St. George's Day. From the Boy Scouts of … to the Boy Scouts of … ' Saint George's Day has been a Scouting event from the beginning. The second edition of The Scout, issued 25th April 1908, was a special 'St. George's Day number'. 'All Scouts should know about St. George,' wrote B.-P. in his leading article. 'St. George is the Patron Saint of England; he is also the Patron Saint of cavalry in all countries, and therefore Patron Saint of the Scouts.'

Photo of a Statuette designed by the Chief Scout and presented by Lord Grey to Canada.

104 This is the style boys liked even better. Baden-Powell made many dozens of sketches of Scout/St. Georges fighting the dragon of evil. This is one of the most striking. In his first Scout newspaper article of April 1908 B.-P. told about the history of St. George, his role in battles during the crusades and the fact that the English flag was based on his red and white colours. 'St. George was typical of what a Scout should be. That is to say, that, when he was faced by a great difficulty or danger, however great it appeared, even in the shape of a dragon, he did not avoid it or fear it, but went at it with all the power he could put into himself and his horse, and, although inadequately armed for such an encounter with merely a sword, he charged in, did his best, and finally succeeded in overcoming the difficulty which nobody had before dared to tackle.'

105 Going around the country, Baden-Powell experienced that the theory of Scouting, as preached in his books and posed on the photocards issued by the Boy Scouts Association, often was far apart from the practice he saw with his own eyes. The drawings and poems he made for the 'Tommy the Tenderfoot series', issued in 1918, show not only his skill in picturing what he had seen, but also how he effected that Scouts would pick up the message and from then on perform better.
No. 1. The Pathfinder does not recognize the tracks to his right and the signs of stones, placed on the road and the cross that tells the experienced tracker that the road straight on should not be followed.
No. 2. Tommy Tenderfoot goes to camp, but has packed his gear the wrong way. A Scout packs everything in a special order, so that the things needed first can be reached easily. A good way of balancing the load makes the trip easier.

106 No. 3. The Camper. Tommy, still carrying the same equipment as on the previous card, arrives in camp and tumbles over the ropes, supporting the tent. A sight that still often can be seen on campings, despite the fact that the tents are lighter (but the ropes often thinner) than in the old days.
Nr. 5. The Bridge Builder. Making lashings and pioneering have become almost an exclusive Scout proficiency during the last decades. In the past builders made scaffoldings with wooden poles and rope-lashings. These heavy and difficult-to-handle materials now have been replaced by lightweight metal poles and practical joints. The know-how of tying the right knots (not only strong, but also easy to untie) and lashings (efficient and safe) has probably yet been forgotten by modern professionals in the building trade.

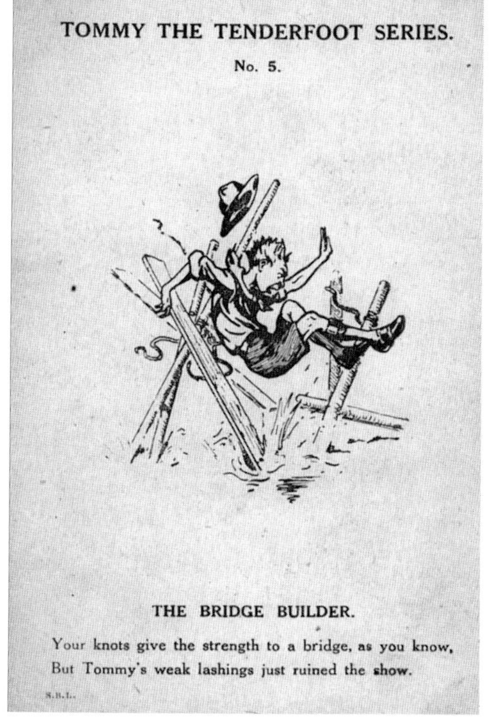

107 No. 4. Fire-lighting. That's another thing that might be forgotten in these days of central heating. In houses with an open fire the trick is often done with special materials like easy-to-light blocks and other fire-makers. A Scout should know ho to do it with the wood he finds and that can be really difficult when it has been raining for a day or more. The Scout in the background knows how to do it.

No. 6. Stalking. That's another thing Tommy is no expert in. Seeing without being seen, that's what it's all about. Baden-Powell had a lot of experience in stalking and the boys liked his talks about the days he had put this skill into practice in India and Africa. 'It is quite a lesson to watch a Zulu Scout making use of a hilltop or rising ground as a look-out place. He will crawl up on all fours, lying flat in the grass; on reaching the top he will very slowly raise his head, inch by inch, till he can see the view.'

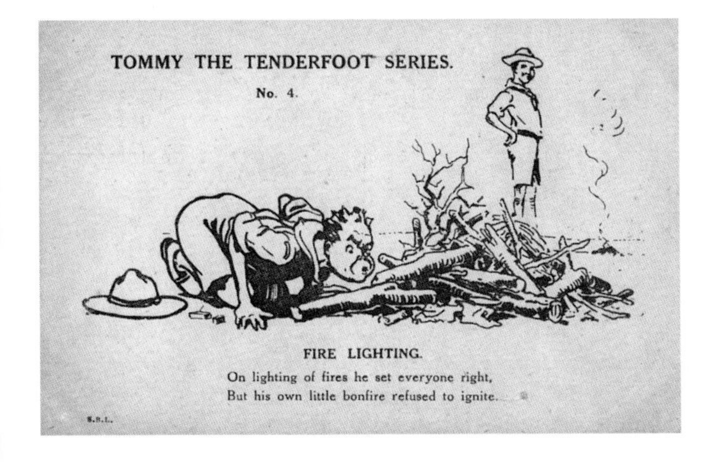

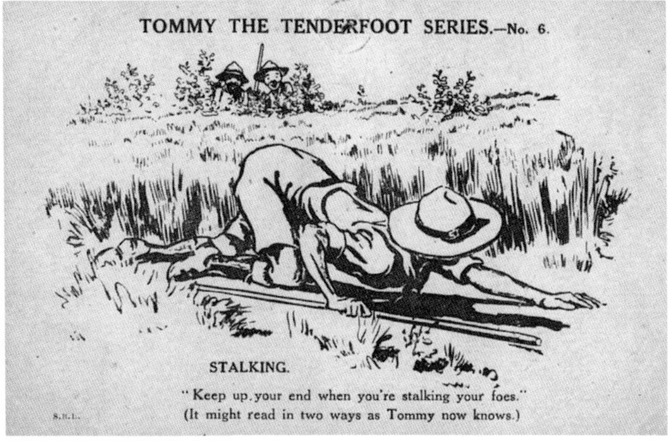

 No. 7. Tommy has forgotten his Scouts' staff. It's a long time since the Scout staff was abandoned. Yet, as we look through the literature of the first years, there were many good uses for this peaceful piece of armament. A tenderfoot had to learn them all. It could be used to keep bystanders back from accidents, to make a tripod to hang a cookingpot over the fire, to act as tentpole, to avert mad dogs, to measure distances and heights, to improvise a stretcher for carrying wounded, to rescue people from the water, to climb walls, etc. The staff was reckoned part of the uniform and without it the boy was no Scout.

No. 9. Tommy as Pioneer. He did not sharpen his axe, and that makes the tool even more dangerous. With a well-sharpened ax you can sharpen a pencil, our Scoutmaster showed and taught us. Carrying the thing around in a safe way is part of the knowledge of a trained Scout. Securely against cutting yourself and avoiding to harm anyone else.

109 No. 8. Tommy is sleeping out and makes the old mistake to pile his blankets on top of himself, forgetting that in camp most cold comes from the ground, not to speak of damp adding to the problem. The trained Scout in the background has organized his bed better. He uses his shoes to support his improvised pillow, a trick B.-P. brought back from his many travels in the Indian and African countryside.

No. 12. Tommy cannot swim. That was not unusual for most people a century ago. There were almost no swimming pools, and no people to teach you. Going into a river was not done and considered dangerous. The fact that many people lived in the big cities, where open water was often filthy, made the chances to learn to swim even smaller. Going into the countryside and learning to swim, made Scouts not only more self-dependent, but gave them the opportunity to save the lives of others. A large number of the medals awarded were for the rescue of people who couldn't swim.

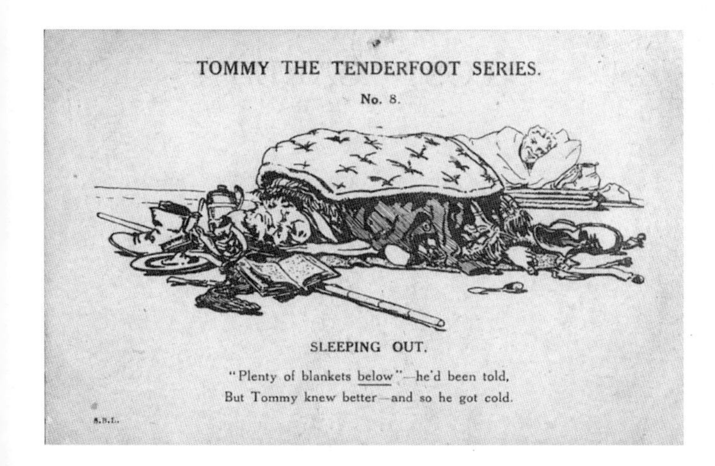

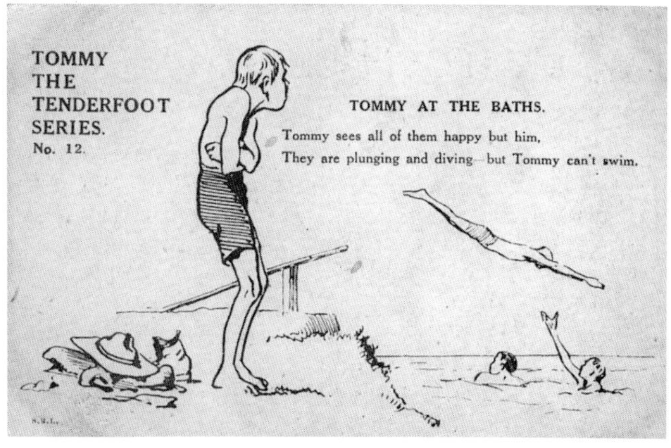

110 The last two cards in the series Baden-Powell designed for his young followers.
No. 10. Tommy is not prepared without his 'haversack'. What a nice, old-fashioned name for the rucksack to carry your camping-gear with you. In the days that the world was unimaginable without horses, a haversack no doubt was a very common thing and easy to come by for any Scout. It took some time before suppliers were ready to offer camping materials and the days that lightweight equipment and carry-more-rucksacks came available still were far off.
No. 11. Tommy is pictured as Mammy's darling. The short trousers Baden-Powell advised his Scouts to wear, were far away from the children's and grown-up's fashion of the time. The old photographs show that most boys had very long short trousers that almost hid their knees completely. The Scoutmasters often didn't dare to expose their legs and stuck to riding-breeches. The winters in England seemed too cold for this and the story was told that dogs loved to bite in the flesh shown on their eye-level.

111 In 1924 another Jamboree was held in connection with the Wembley Empire Exhibition. This Imperial Jamboree was designed along the same lines as the one at Olympia, but in view of the nature of the Exhibition, emphasis was laid on the Imperial side rather than on the International. 12,500 Scouts from all corners of the British Commonwealth came to Wembley to take part in the camp. A highlight of the Jamboree was the visit of the Prince of Wales, dressed in Scout uniform. This card pictures the Prince and Baden-Powell inspecting the British Representative Troop at the Stadium, before they sailed to Copenhagen, Danmark, to take part in the World's International Scouting Contests, part of the program of the 2nd World Jamboree, held that same summer. When Scoutmaster C.V. Swan, M.C. saw this postcard, he will have been disappointed, because he has been spotted out almost completely. Only his legs can be seen behind those of the Chief Scout for Wales.

H.R.H. THE PRINCE OF WALES AND SIR BADEN POWELL INSPECTING BOY SCOUTS.

112 It's time to leave the Boy Scouts for a while and show a number of postcards picturing the Girl Guides. We have already seen that the Girl Guides Association, started in 1910, worked principally along the same lines as their brothers did. The first years, under the leadership of Agnes Baden-Powell, the Victorian influence could be felt, but during the First World War the girls worked like men to help their country and the new feeling of self-assertion brought about a change in the leadership. The much younger Lady Baden-Powell took the reins and modernized the fastly-growing movement. This card and the following two date from 1921 and are a choice from a series dedicated to the Llangattock School of Arts and Crafts for Crippled Girls, Heritage Craft Schools, Chailey, Sussex.

PRINCESS LOUISE'S OWN HERITAGE COMPANY OF GIRL GUIDES.

113 In the 1920's troops were established for handicapped girls and boys, especially at schools for the blind, deaf and dumb and crippled children. The Girl Guides can be proud to have been the pioneers in this field. Here we see the Guide Company and the Brownie Pack of 'Princess Louise's Own Heritage Company', at the Llangattock School of Arts and Crafts for Crippled Girls at Chailey, Sussex. At that moment the company numbered some fifty Guides, who had their own headquarters – former army huts – near the school. The Brownie Pack, some twenty strong, is pictured in 'The Clump', the crops nearby, with their totem, a toadstool, in the centre. The company was named after Princess Louise, who took a great interest in Guiding and was, from 1911 till 1939, the first patron of the Girl Guides Association.

114 The National Centre for the Girl Guides was the building pictured on these two cards. Foxlease, in the New Forest, was given to the Girl Guide's Association in 1922 by Mrs. Archbold, the American owner, to serve as a camping place and a national training centre. The upkeep of the place was made possible by the Association's President, Princess Mary, who donated £6,000 of her wedding present for equipping and endowing. In the summer of 1924 a World Camp was organized in and around Foxlease. There had been international conferences before that year, where only guiders were present, but this time the girls from many countries came to England to take part in the camp. Of the 1,100 participants 600 came from abroad.

115 Guiding was introduced in existing organizations as a basis for their youth work. The Y.W.C.A. for instance, had Girl Guide Companies all over the country. The Salvation Army developed its own system, introducing companies of 'Guards' who, instead of the well-known dark-blue uniform werd dressed in gray dresses, trimmed with purple collar and cuffs. They did not feel the need to be part of the Girl Guides Association and their own organization of Salvation Army Scouts and Guards was not only active on the British Isles, but also in other parts of the Empire and on the continent of Europe. Child Nurse was one of the most popular proficiency badges a Girl Guide could earn. This card, No. 203 in the series 'Young People of the Army', shows us a practical lesson.

116 Helping on a farm was another thing Girl Guides practised. This postcard with a 1920 photograph, shows the traditional equipment used in those days. Several Girl Guide badges could be gained at the farm or in the country. Basket Maker, Bee Keeper, Dairy Worker, Friend to Animals, Gardener, Handywoman, Landgirl, Poultry Farmer and Rabbit Keeper are a few of the many possibilities. A Landgirl wore a badge with a sickle and had assisted in some form of landwork for at least eight days, looked after cattle for at least a month, knew something about two breeds of cattle, pigs or sheep and one breed of horses in her area, and their special uses. She had shown knowledge of the arable cropping of her district and could describe a farming year and she knew the part played by six or more implements in farm work, like the plough, harrow, Cambridge roller, flat roller, seed-drill, manure distributor, horseshoe, reaper and binder, mowing machine, tedder or swathe turner, horse-rake, hay-fork, and hay-rake.

117 The text on the reverse side of this card reads 'Installations de cuisine', which reveals that we are in France. Like the Boy Scouts, Girl Guiding had spread overseas and this card, which we guess is from the 1930's, shows us the camp kitchen built by members of the 'Fédération Française des Eclaireuses'. Girl Guides are masters in camp building and make one feel at home. Look at this efficient kitchen. First of all there's a roof over the fire, shielding it against rain. The tripod in front of the shelter is a practical wash-stand. In the background there's a handy table with room to store pots, pans, plates, cutlery, etc. Girl Guides serve camp menus that can compete with multistar restaurants. An efficient kitchen not only results in safe and tasty food, it also saves time for other camping opportunities.

118 This is the last card in our short Girl Guide series. It's a pity that we haven't space enough to picture more old Guide cards form England or abroad, but, who knows, there comes an opportunity to make a separate book 'Girl Guides in old picture postcards' in due course. The card here is of French origin also. It pictures the Guides of the Roman Catholic boarding school Sophia at Ajmer, Rajasthan, India. It's a well-dressed and obviously well-drilled company, the mission of the 'Capucins Français aux Indes' have organized. We guess that the card dates from the thirties. Scouting in the colonies was registered internationally through the home country, be that Britain, France or another nation. In 1948 India was welcomed as a separate member of the WAGGGS, the World Association of Girl Guides and Girl Scouts. With Israel it was one of the first to have one association for boys and girls.

119 We go back to the boys. It is 1929. Scouting celebrates its coming-of-age with the biggest World Jamboree ever held. This view from an aeroplane of the opening ceremony shows us the arena where the 50,000 Scouts from some seventy countries have gathered. In the background we see the tented city. After the 1920 and 1924 World Jamborees this 3rd great international camp was held after a five-year interval, not only to fit in with the coming-of-age, but also to get out of the way of the Olympic Games, that were growing in numbers as well as in press-attention. Baden-Powell had seen how the acorn he planted in 1907 at Brownsea Island had grown into a massive oak. The idea was to choose Great Britain, the founder country, to host the Jamboree. The Mayor and Corporation of Birkenhead offered the use of Arrowe Park, 450 acres, with a Hall for conferences, excellent travelling facilities and a port for those coming by sea.

A view from an aeroplane of the opening of the great International Jamboree at Arrowe Park, Birkenhead, England, 1929.
Price One Penny. Photo by "Daily Dispatch," Manchester and London

120 With Greetings from the World Jamboree, Arrowe Park, Birkenhead, says this card, designed by Baden-Powell himself and sold by the Scout Shop. The name of the park inspired the Scouts of course. The arrowhead, pointing the right way on any map, had been their symbol and badge from the beginning. The Jamboree badge, to be worn by all participants to serve as an admission ticket and as a souvenir, showed the golden arrow. The editor of The Scout, the national Scout weekly, F. Haydn Dimmock, took care that the huge camp had its own newspaper. The 30,000 copies of 'The Daily Arrowe' were sold out rapidly on the first day of the camp, so the circulation had to be enlarged. 'The main great object of this camp is that you should meet your brother Scouts of different nations and MAKE FRIENDS with them. Don't forget this, and don't waste any time in starting to do it,' wrote B.-P. in the first issue of the Daily Arrowe.

121 Let's have a walk through the 1929 World Jamboree Camp. We are helped by a selection of postcards, made and issued by the French Scouts magazine afterwards. This World Camp was quite different from the first one in 1920 and the Imperial Jamboree of 1924. These were staged demonstrations for the general public, with the Scouts, the artists and performers, camping nearby. The young Danish organizers of the 2nd World Jamboree at Copenhagen in 1924, had a new formula: a great city of tents, where the public was welcome to see the Scouts in their contingent camps and watch their demonstrations in the arena. The difference can be seen in these two cards, picturing the very nice gate erected by the Scouts from Yorkshire, Sheffield and West Riding. Note the many smoking chimneys: then they symbolised prosperity, not pollution, as they would today. Among the many types of tents the French ones stand out because they are painted with colourful patrol animals and troop symbols.

122 The 320,000 visitors of the 1929 World Jamboree were welcome in the camp of the 'Boy Scouts of America'. So were the Scouts of the world and this gate does not make a secret of this hospitality. 'The Scouts of America have sent 1,500 Scouts to the Jamboree from all parts of America,' the Daily Arrowe told. 'As you walk round their camp you will find real Red Indian "teepees" and Scouts in full war paint practising weird Indian dances; Scouts who are experts at fire-lighting with the fire-drill; others cooking national dishes over their fires. You will see from their "Merit Badges" what all-round Scouts they are. Most of them will also be wearing a much-coveted badge, the "Eagle Scout", which is the equivalent of our King's Scout Badge. (...) It is interesting to remember that it was through a good turn done by a British Scout to an American gentleman in 1909 that the Boy Scouts of America started their Movement, which now numbers over 814,000.'

123 It is difficult, even impossible, to illustrate the story of the 1929 World Jamboree, the biggest ever, in a few picture postcards. Perhaps this one here catches the circumstances better than any other. The Scouts who attended this historic gathering remember it as the 'Mudboree'. Chief Scout Baden-Powell didn't expect anything else. In the first Daily Arrowe he wrote: 'The title which I won for myself at the Copenhagen Jamboree and again at the Rally in Budapest was that of BATHING MASTER, because I brought down a downpour of rain on each occasion. I expect it will be the same at Arrowe Park – so Be Prepared for it. Don't expect to be made comfortable in camp. Any comfort that you need must be made by yourselves. You will get lots of discomforts and disappointments, and I know you will take them all in the right spirit.'

124 A Scout is always busy, when he is camping. At a Jamboree he is more busy than ever. Making friends with 50,000 brother Scouts in a fortnight is no small task. On the other hand, those at home expect a letter from the son, brother, nephew or neighbour who is having the time of his life. This big problem was solved by the Daily Mail. In the camp centre their marquee was equipped with tables, pencils and free cards to send home. You only had to cross out the words not required and, unless this example here has not been used, one can imagine what words were crossed out to describe the weather. The Daily Arrowe showed how delivery vans got stuck in the mud, needing petrol and B.-P. spirit (human) to get free.

CAMP POST CARD

SENT FROM THE "DAILY MAIL" MARQUEE.

CROSS OUT WORDS NOT REQUIRED.

I am feeling fine and enjoying myself.

The weather is fine. fair. bad.

I have / have not received your letter. / parcel.

I have been / am going on an Excursion. / to the Camp Theatre. / to the Camp Cinema.

I shall be writing a letter shortly.

....

Signature.

125 The 1929 World Jamboree brought many honours and presents to Baden-Powell. The King marked this signal event in the Scouting history by conferring a peerage on the Chief Scout, who chose to be called Lord Baden-Powell of Gilwell. The Prince of Wales spent the night of 1st August in camp. His Royal Highness took the march-past in front of the royal box in the vast stadium the next afternoon. The Scouts of the World had contributed a penny each to provide B.-P. with a coming-of-age gift. Never were pennies so cheerfully given; the difficulty was to refuse their offers of more. The birthday fund was devoted to a portrait of B.-P. by David Jagger and to a Rolls-Royce and Eccles caravan. At the closing day of the Jamboree, B.-P. distributed replicas of the camp symbol, the Golden Arrow, to all contingent leaders as a sign of peace, goodwill and fellowship.

126 This postcard pictures a 'permanent Jamboree': the International Scout Chalet at Kandersteg, Switzerland. In 1923 this former hostel for workers on the Lötschberg tunnel was turned into a hostel for Scouts. Generous donors, notably Mortimer L. Schiff of the Boy Scouts of America, enabled the International Scout Chalet Association in 1929 to buy a large tract of land on which the debris from the tunnel had been spread. Gradually this stony ground has been covered with earth and trees and provides a variety of camp sites and also a training centre for the Swiss Scout Association. In 1926 Kandersteg was host to the 4th International Conference. The International Committee held a meeting there in 1930. And World Rover Moots (Jamborees for Scouts over 18) were held there in 1931 and 1953. Every year the Scouts Alpine Club organizes courses in skiing and climbing.

Internationales Pfadfinderheim. Home international d'éclaireurs
Scouts' International Châlet. Stabile internazionale dei Giovani Esploratori.
Kandersteg. Berner Oberland. Schweiz.

127 The 22th of February is a day on which Scouts and Guides the world over remember the two Chiefs. Lord and Lady Baden-Powell shared the same birthday and especially the Girl Guides transformed this day into 'Thinking Day', an occasion to send greetings on special postcards to each other around the world and to do a special good turn towards International Guiding. The Chief Scout himself was more in favour of Saint George's Day instead of receiving attention to his person. But the joint birthdays made it difficult and yet impossible to leave him out of the spotlights altogether. The couple received loads of good wishes from all over the world and these were responded to with a self-made card. This one dates from 1925: the milestone shows the Chief's age.

128 A special and interesting collection can be made of cards designed by the Chief Scout. Most of them have been printed on solid cardboard and in large numbers. They can be separated into at least three categories: Christmas/New Year wishes, Birthday wishes and Others. This card belongs to the last category and shows a picture puzzle that is typical for B.-P.'s sense of humour and his skill as an artist. The original of this card measures 143 x 105 mm and could be mailed as a postcard, as the reverse has separate spaces for address and writing. The precise date of making is unknown.

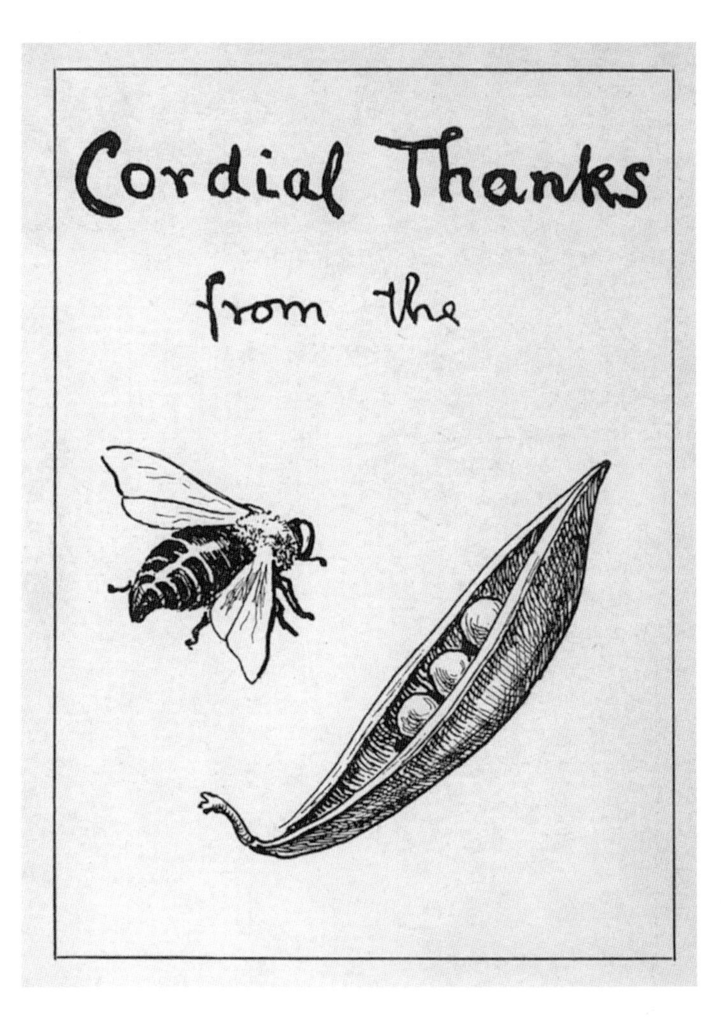

129 The B.-P. family (complete with the two dogs) is portrayed on this 1933-1934 Season's greetings card. The photo on the left shows the two Chiefs and their three children aboard a ship of the White Star Line during a trip to the Baltic countries. The S.S. Calgaric had been hired for the purpose and sailed on 12th August 1933 from Southampton with 620 Scouters and Guiders for a seventeen-day tour. They went to Rotterdam, then eastwards through the Kiel Canal and cruised round the Baltic capital cities, returning by the Skagerrak to Oslo and thence to Liverpool, a round trip of some 3,500 miles. At each place the party was welcomed and entertained by and received into the homes of the Scout and Guide people of those countries. The original is much larger than the usual postcard: 153 x 229 mm and it needed an envelope to be mailed.

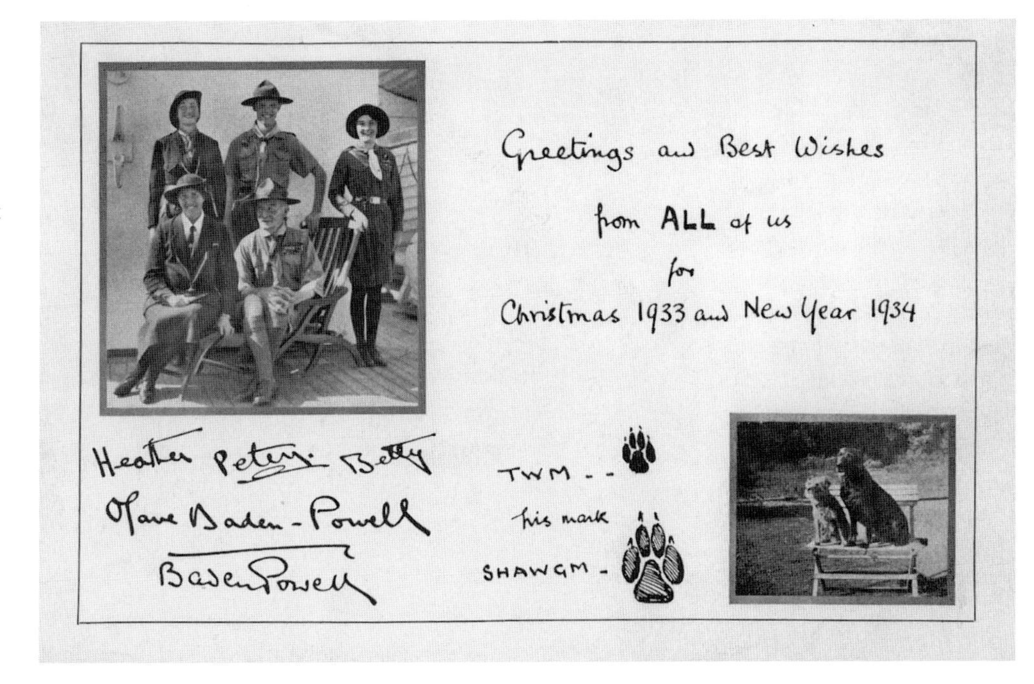

130 This thank-you card pictures the family in 1937. It shows that the children have grown up quickly in the past few years. On 22th February 1937 the Chiefs celebrated their 80th and 48th birthday and in October they had been married for 25 years. The B.-P.'s had become grandparents twice. Their son Peter (1913) had joined the British South Africa Police. He married Carine Crause Boardman. Their son Robert was born in October 1936. The youngest daughter Betty (1917) had married Gervas Clay. They lived in Northern Rhodesia and in June 1937 their daughter Gillian was born. Heather Baden-Powell (1915) married Pilot Officer John King, RAFVR in 1940.

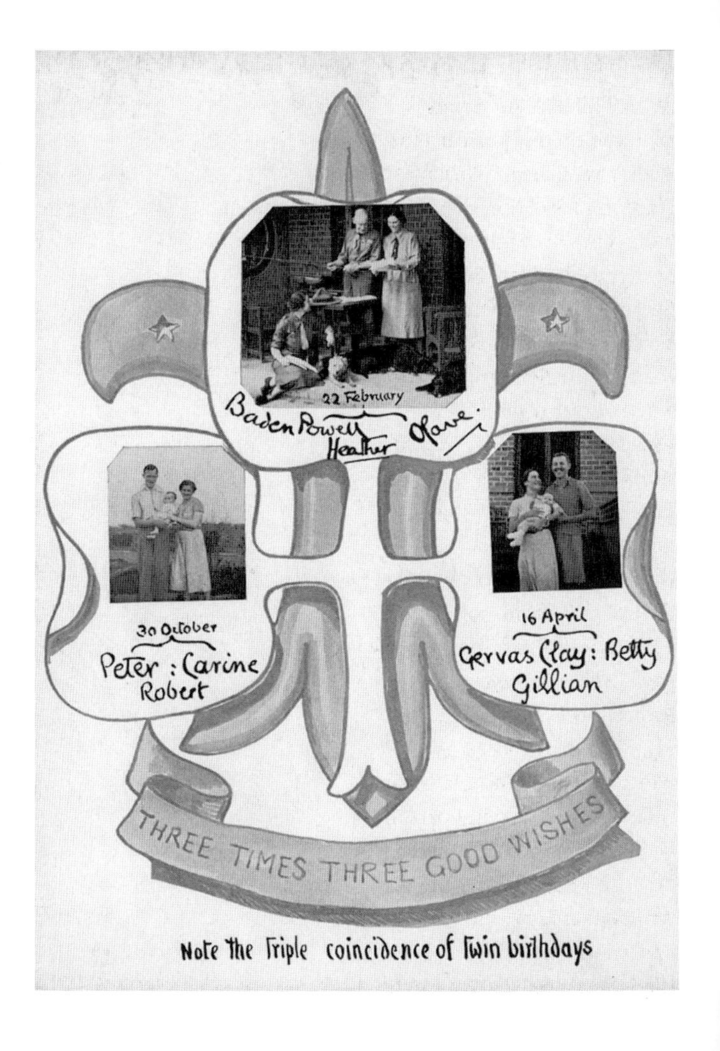

131 This card takes us back to 1935. The Chief Scout is pictured on this postcard together with Prince Gustav Adolph of Sweden. The occasion is the Rover Moot, held at Ingarö, Sweden. Before the Second World War there were several other Royal Scouts in many countries, ranging from King Farouk (Egypt), King Charles II (Romania), King Boris (Bulgaria) to princes in Liechtenstein, Italy, Greece and other countries. Some of these were patron of the national association, some wore a Scout uniform at certain occasions, but few were as active as the Swedish Crown Prince. The Jamboree of 1929 had proved that too many too old Scouts kept taking part in an event meant for younger boys. In 1931 a Rover Moot was held at Kandersteg, with a program specially designed for Scouts-over-18. Four years later the Swedish Scouts hosted the 2nd World Rover Moot with Prince Gustav Adolph as camp chief. Two years later he became chairman of the Scouts World Committee.

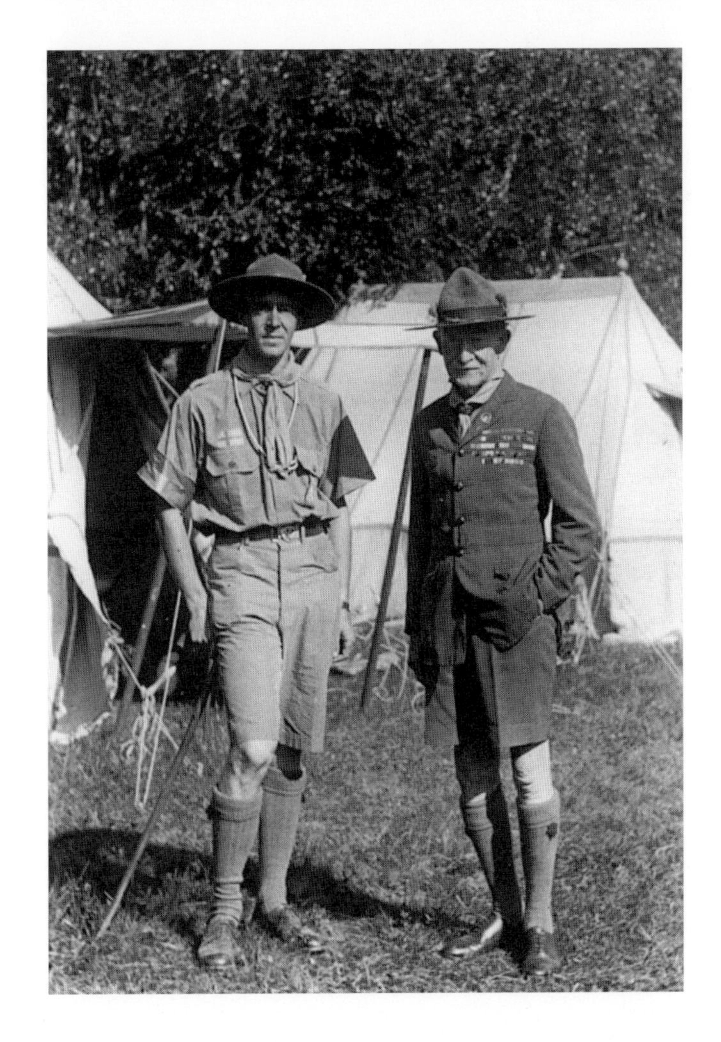

132 The Duke and Duchess of York had been supporting Scouting and Guiding in England for many years. This postcard, issued by J. Beagles & Co. Ltd. from London, dates from 1936. The Duke had been Commodore for Sea Scouts and after his coronation in May 1937 he received the King's Scouts at Windsor for the first time. In the 1930's a training and employment scheme was started by the Boy Scouts to train unemployed men, preferably Rover Scouts, from the distressed areas, for private service as butlers, cooks, valets, footmen, houseboys, chauffeurs, gardeners and handymen. The success was amazing, so the Ministry of Labour gave its support. New training centres were opened. In 1936 the scheme received Royal Patronage and in July of that year the Duke and Duchess visited one of the centres.

133 Shortly after the coronation the Girl Guides welcomed two new recruits. The 1st Buckingham Palace Company was started in the Palace schoolroom. 'You will find them just like ordinary girls,' the governess ('Crawfie') had ensured the Guider appointed to be Captain of the new unit. At the first acquaintance Princess Margaret escaped from the nursery and pleaded to be accepted as a member too. So from the start not only a company of Guides had to be formed, but also a pack of Brownies. On the postcard we see Princess Elisabeth as second of the Kingfisher Patrol and her sister Margaret as a member of the Leprechaun-six. The photograph was taken at Windsor Castle just before the march-past of the King's Scouts. Standing on the left is Princess Mary, active in Guiding since 1917 and Patron of the Girl Guides Association since 1920.

134 It is Saturday 31st July 1937. In Vogelenzang near Haarlem in Holland the 5th World Jamboree is opened by a march-past of 27,000 Scouts from over fifty countries. This would be the last Jamboree for the 80-year old Chief Scout. The boys felt this and they had come to the Jamboree in larger numbers than the organizers had imagined. At the grand stand Queen Wilhelmina's Royal Standard is flying. At this moment the British contingent marches past in rows of ten with flags flying. The parade lasted for over an hour. The weather was fine, quite contrary to some of the past rallies Baden-Powell attended. To the right part of the press platform can be seen. The camp received much press covering. Newspapers, magazines and radio programs payed attention to this world camp. The Jamboree song was a hit: 'Jamboree, Jamboree, J-A-M-B-O-R-E-E, we are the Scouts of Chief B.-P. !'

135 Queen Wilhelmina visited the World Jamboree twice. Here we see the grand stand on 5th August 1937, while the Dutch Wolf Cubs stage a big demonstration of their many skills. Note the Scout badge on the hat of the Queen. It's the golden badge that her late husband Prince Henry used to wear when he was in Scout uniform. At the right hand of the Queen we see B.-P. (wearing the Grand Cross of Orange Nassau) and the Dutch Chief Scout Admiral Rambonnet. At her left hand Prince Gustav Adolph (Sweden) and Prince Bernhard. The latter was introduced to Scouting by the Swedish Prince, with the result that he succeeded the old Admiral as chairman of the Dutch Scouts one year later. In the second row we see Lady Baden-Powell. The Dutch Girl Guides took the opportunity to meet the Chief Guide. The opening march-past was preceded by a large number of Dutch Guides in her honour.

136 The World Jamboree in Holland is a rich source for collectors of picture post-cards. Over two hundred cards were issued, most of them photos, picturing all sorts of camp activities, for-eign uniforms and official moments. Sponsoring manu-facturers showed Scouts using their products, ranging from canned vegetables and choc-olate to typewriters and mouth organs. And some for-eign contingents had their own souvenir cards ready. One of the most rare ones is pictured here. The back shows the text: 'Greetings from the "Brownsea Troop". In the summer of 1907, the Chief held his first experimental Scout Camp on Brownsea Island, Poole, Dorset. From the acorn thus planted the oak has grown whose branches now spread over the whole world.'

137 In a quiet corner of the big and crowded World Jamboree we find the camp of the British contingent staff. This photo shows, from left to right: Lt.Col. C.W. Becking, hon. treasurer of the World Jamboree, Capt. C. Boyle, secretary to the Boy Scouts Association, Lord Somers, acting Chief Scout and leader of the British contingent to the World Jamboree, Gen. Maj. b.d. H. Behrens, deputy chairman of the World Jamboree. The 6,000-strong British contingent (the largest ever taken overseas till then) consisted of Scouts from Australia, New Zealand, South Africa, Ireland, New Foundland, British India, Barbados, Bermuda, British Guiana, Ceylon, Hong Kong, Jamaica, Malta, Northern Rhodesia, Palestina, Trinidad, and British troops from Belgium, Egypt, France, Switzerland and of course England, Scotland, Wales and Northern Ireland.

138 The closing ceremony of the 5th World Jamboree was a memorable and moving moment. After a final march-past the 27,000 Scouts gathered round the platform with the old Chief Scout. A tense silence – then the Chief began to speak: 'We have come to the end of our Jamboree... We have been called a boys' crusade, the Crusade of Peace, and it is a very apt description of our Scout Brotherhood...' After the presentation of the camp totems, the Jacob's Staff, to all leaders of national contingents, the Chief continued: 'Now the time has come for me to say good-bye. I want you to lead happy lives. You know that many of us will never meet again in this world. I am in my eighty-first year and am nearing the end of my life. Most of you are at the beginning and I want your lives to be happy and successful. You can make them so by doing your best to carry out the Scout Law all your days, whatever your station and wherever you are... Now good-bye. God bless you all.'

139 That same evening the Scouts gathered for the last time around the campfire with their founder. The Chief Scout was seated in a comfortable armchair, constructed by the Rover Scouts of the working party. On his right hand we see Prince Gustav Adolph. Next to him Dr. James E. West, Chief Scout Executive of the Boy Scouts of America, and Hubert Martin, Director of the Boy Scouts International Bureau. In the front row from the right Princess Juliana (with dark bonnet), at her left hand (only partly seen) Lady Baden-Powell. At her right hand Mrs. Rambonnet (wife of the Dutch Chief Scout), Prince Bernhard of the Netherlands, Mr. J. Roëll (Royal Court functionary) and Col. John S. Wilson (Chief Gilwell Park and – on occasions like this – bodyguard to B.-P.). At the end of the year 1937 Baden-Powell sailed to Kenya, where he died in 1941.

140 The end of the Jamboree. The end of this book. But not the end of Scouting. The Second World War did not leave the movement untouched. In most of the occupied countries Scouting was forbidden and went underground. After the war Scouting came back, but in the East-European countries not for long. A new and long period of suppression followed till 1989, when the Iron Curtain came down. The total numbers of the Scout movement in 1939 were 3,3 million; in 1998 there are over 25 million Scouts in 216 countries and territories. Add to this that some 25 countries are registered through a (mother-) country and that recently-formed associations in about forty countries are working towards official registration, then it's clear that Scouting is still growing in strength. To these can be added the numbers of the Girl Guides and Girl Scouts. They have nearly 10 million members in 136 countries. And that all began with a trial camp of twenty English boys and a book written by a genius: Baden-Powell.